HEALING MIRACLES

EDGAR CAYCE'S WISDOM FOR THE NEW AGE

General Editor: Charles Thomas Cayce
Project Editor: A. Robert Smith

HEALING MIRACLES

Using Your Body Energies

WILLIAM A. McGAREY, M.D.

With a Foreword by Charles Thomas Cayce

1817

Harper & Row, Publishers, San Francisco

Cambridge, Hagerstown, New York, Philadelphia, Washington
London, Mexico City, São Paulo, Singapore, Sydney

FIRST EDITION

Library of Congress Cataloging-in-Publication Data

McGarey, William A.
  Healing miracles.

  (Edgar Cayce's wisdom for the new age)
  Bibliography: p.
  Includes index.
  1. Alternative medicine.   I. Title.   II. Series
R733.M39 1988   615.5   88-45146
ISBN 0-06-250588-2 (pbk.)

88 89 90 91 92 FG 10 9 8 7 6 5 4 3 2 1

CONTENTS

ACKNOWLEDGMENTS

I WISH TO ACKNOWLEDGE ALL those who have been instrumental in the compilation of this manuscript and all those who have shared their experiences with me over the years:

Hugh Lynn Cayce
Gladys T. McGarey
Peggy K. Grady
Harvey Grady
Erika Bauer
June Newton
Bill and Elsie Sechrist
Maxine Aten
Stella Andres
John B. McGarey
Doctors J. D. and Heather McClary
Bob Smith

and especially Edgar Cayce, who made all these experiences in healing the body possible!

FOREWORD

I$_T$ $_{IS}$ $_A$ $_{TIME}$ in the earth when people everywhere seek to know more of the mysteries of the mind, the soul," said my grandfather, Edgar Cayce, from an unconscious trance from which he demonstrated a remarkable gift for clairvoyance.

His words are prophetic even today, as more and more Americans in these unsettled times are turning to psychic explanations for daily events. For example, according to a national survey by the National Opinion Research Council nearly half of American adults today believe they have been in contact with someone who has died, a figure twice that of ten years ago. Two-thirds of all adults say they have had an ESP experience; ten years ago that figure was only one-half.

Every culture throughout history has made note of its own members' gifted powers beyond the five senses. These rare individuals held special interest because they seemed able to provide solutions to life's pressing problems. America in the twentieth century is no exception.

Edgar Cayce was perhaps the most famous and most carefully documented psychic of our time. He began to use his unusual abilities when he was a young man, and from then on for over forty years he would, usually twice a day, lie on a couch, go into a sleeplike state, and respond to questions. Over fourteen thousand of these discourses, called readings, were carefully transcribed by his secretary and preserved by the Edgar Cayce Foundation in Virginia Beach, Virginia. These psychic readings continue to provide inspiration, insight, and help with healing to tens of thousands of people.

Having only an eighth-grade education, Edgar Cayce lived a plain, simple life by the world's standards. As early as his childhood in Hopkinsville, Kentucky, however, he sensed that he had psychic ability. While alone one day he had a vision of a woman who told him he would have unusual power to help people. He also related experiences of "seeing" dead relatives. Once, while struggling with school lessons, he slept on his spelling book and awakened knowing the entire contents of the book.

As a young man he experimented with hypnosis to treat a recurring throat problem that caused him to lose his speech. He discovered that under hypnosis he could diagnose and describe treatments for the physical ailments of others, often without knowing or seeing the person with the ailment. People began to ask him other sorts of questions, and he found himself able to answer these as well.

In 1910 the *New York Times* published a two-page story with pictures about Edgar Cayce's psychic ability as described by a young physician, Wesley Ketchum, to a clinical research society in Boston. From that time on people from all over the country with every conceivable question sought his help.

In addition to his unusual talents, Cayce was a deeply religious man who taught Sunday school all of his adult life and read the entire Bible once for every year that he lived. He always tried to attune himself to God's will by studying the Scriptures and maintaining a rich prayer life, as well as by trying to be of service to those who came seeking help. He used his talents only for helpful purposes. Cayce's simplicity and humility and his commitment to doing good in the world continue to attract people to the story of his life and work and to the far-reaching information he gave.

In this series we hope to provide the reader with insights in the search for understanding and meaning in life. Each book in the series explores its subject from the viewpoint of the Edgar Cayce readings and compares the perspectives of other metaphysical literature and of current scientific thought. The interested reader needs no prior knowledge of the Cayce information. When one of the Edgar Cayce readings is quoted, the identifying number of that reading is included for those who may wish to read the full text. Each volume includes suggestions for further study.

This book, *Healing Miracles: Using Your Body Energies*, by William A. McGarey, M.D., covers the information contained in the thousands of medical readings Edgar Cayce gave. No one is more highly qualified than Dr. McGarey, who has made a study of these readings and applied the medical information found there in treating his own patients for many years at the Association for Research and Enlightenment (A.R.E.) Clinic in Phoenix, Arizona. The many healings accomplished at the Clinic for patients who found little relief from conventional medicine is a tribute not only to the author and his staff but to the continuing value of the unconventional remedies found in the Cayce readings and the soundness of Edgar Cayce's philosophy of healing the body, mind, and spirit.

Charles Thomas Cayce, Ph.D.
President
Association for Research and Enlightenment

PREFACE

SOME TWENTY-FIVE HUNDRED YEARS ago, Patanjali, the first of the great Yoga teachers, delivered a treatise on the nature of the world and the nature of human beings. From one side, he described the cosmos as organized in structured layers of Mind called matter, emotions, mind, and spirit. From the other, he talked of how the individual might become conscious of the cosmos, in every dimension, and he spoke of how to work in the cosmos.

Patanjali's fundamental concept is, Everything consists of Mind and its modifications. In his view, the cosmos, with all its parts—galaxies, solar systems, planets, people—is an expression of Mind. Further, each human being is a spark of mind, living life after life in a developmental journey, destined for full expression of light, love, and power, that is, knowledge, compassion, and strength.

As a student in the Department of Physics at the University of Minnesota, when I had begun to understand Patanjali's concepts, I came across Thomas Sugrue's book *There Is a River*. The story of Edgar Cayce's development into an embodiment of love was fascinating, of itself, but most interesting from a scientific viewpoint was the cluster of ideas relating to Mind and matter, what the human mind is, how mind works within the body, how it works in interpersonal relations, how it works in finding creative solutions to intellectual problems, and how it works in finding, and expressing, Mind.

By perseverance and pondering, I translated some of Cayce's difficult language into relatively simple English, and I was impressed to find that Cayce's ideas were essentially the same as Patanjali's, namely:

> *There is only one nature.* Its laws do not change. Being seers, both Patanjali and Cayce described the same nature and the same Mind, but from different viewpoints. Parallels are also found in the writings of the teachers who sponsored H. P. Blavatsky and the Theosophical Society.
>
> *All phenomena—mental, emotional, and physical—follow natural law.* There are no miracles. Nothing is supernatural. There are only spiritual processes, and these are "natural." Jesus said about his healings and other unusual events, "These things shall ye do." He seemed to be saying, as presaged by Patanjali and echoed by Cayce, that each person has full "potential," though undeveloped.
>
> *There is only one Mind.* Every individual mind, whether conscious of it or not, is a part of that one Mind.
>
> *The energy of nature is the energy of Mind.* Everything is constructed of, and is constructed by, Mind. To change nature, within or without the body, you must change Mind. To accomplish this intentionally it is necessary to align oneself with Mind, to be able to think in Mind. Then, results within the body and in nature are automatic and inevitable.

It is illuminating to find that the leading spiritual teachers have these same ideas. Aurobindo, in *The Synthesis of Yoga*, covers the same ground as Patanjali and Cayce, but in a different way and with his own vocabulary. In Alice Ann Bailey's book *The Treatise on White Magic*, her teacher, the Tibetan, reveals the same grand picture of cosmos, hierarchy, and humanity in another vocabulary. Manly Palmer Hall shows the same picture again in his *Secret Teachings of All Ages: An Encyclopedic Outline of Masonic, Hermetic, Cabalistic, and Rosicrucian Philosophy*. My wife, Alyce, and I received the same view of Mind and nature from a teacher whom we first met in the late 1930s. The teacher's instruction included: Do not accept these ideas of human mind, universal Mind, and the cosmos on faith; test them. Do not believe or disbelieve; those emotional states are impediments. Remember, and test. Try it in life. *Know* what you are talking about, for belief is then superseded. Meditate and practice self-regulation, and you will move toward understanding. Is it not remarkable that this, in essence, is the Cayce teaching, and is the teaching of Drs. William and Gladys McGarey?

On the other hand, perhaps it is not really remarkable to have seers agree on what *is*. They may have different eyes and different perspectives, but they seem to view the same multidimensional universe. If they truly "see," it would be more remarkable to find them in disagreement.

With these ideas, we now have a yardstick with which to judge the hundreds of books and inner development courses and cassette tapes that have deluged us in the 1980s on mysticism, occultism, spiritism, channeling, self-power, subliminal programming, and so on. If these things contradict Patanjali, Cayce, the Tibetan, Aurobindo, the Teacher, we put them aside. If they agree in part, we value them in part. If they correspond in principles, even though focusing on new scientific data and expressing new cultural viewpoints, we absorb them. Our amalgam, if it could be complete, would describe Mind and nature, and also would describe our part, as human beings, in unfolding the Plan of the teachers.

I hope everyone who reads this book will *think* about what it means, *intuit* what it means, and *apply* what it means. These three things were stressed by Edgar Cayce over the years, and Dr. McGarey has given us much material from his experience with the Cayce readings and their application to help us understand mind. The author does not say he is a theoretician, but he is a practitioner, a tester of ideas, a searcher after meanings, and he has distilled for us his experience with the Cayce material over the last quarter century.

This book was valuable to me. It substantiated and reinforced my understanding of the nature of Nature. In reading it, I made an effort to maintain an intuitive mental stance, absorbing it and allowing the basic ideas to form themselves first in the unconscious, and then in the conscious. From this, it took shape as one of the perennial visions of Mind.

So, in studying this record of clinical experience, it is appropriate again to say, "*Think, intuit,* and *apply.*"

Elmer E. Green, Ph.D.
Director
Voluntary Controls Program
The Menninger Foundation

INTRODUCTION

MODERN AMERICAN MEDICINE FACES a serious crisis. Over the past forty years, hospital and health care insurance has become a major industry, with constantly rising costs to the consumer. The skyrocketing cost of medical malpractice insurance and legal services for malpractice lawsuits threatens the continuation of many aspects of medical care. At the same time, the public has become increasingly disenchanted with the medical profession, which for so many years enjoyed its place high on a pedestal. Despite the term *health care*, the greater portion of the medical profession does not care for the health of patients. Rather, most efforts are aimed at patients' illnesses—the pathology—after they have lost their health.

The question that has perplexed me over the forty-five years I have spent in the profession is, Why has the conquest of disease been so elusive and prevention so inadequate?

It is true that advances have been made. Polio, tuberculosis, and the childhood infectious diseases have been controlled to a large extent. But we've suffered setbacks too. Childhood cancer has increased, and candidiases, hypoglycemia, Epstein-Barr virus syndrome, and acquired immune deficiency syndrome (AIDS) have all appeared in the last two or three decades.

Why is it that when we supposedly conquer one disease another takes its place? Why can we not take an individual who has a failing heart and restore it back to normal without open-heart surgery or organ transplant? Why do we not recognize that the normal condition of the human being is an abundant state of health? And why is it that we cannot, or at least *have not*, recognized and dealt with the factors that really bring about a state of disharmony or illness? These are some of the questions that need to be explored and answered before the public is going to be satisfied that they are being dealt with honestly and constructively.

Some of the most comprehensive approaches to many of these questions can be found in the lifework of the American mystic Edgar Cayce, who died the year after I entered medical school. I have studied extensively in the nearly fifteen thousand readings he gave and applied his unconventional remedies on my patients over many years. This book is about Cayce's concepts, which lie behind those remedies, and how helpful they have proved to be.

Cayce's desire, even as a child, was to help people. And it was only lack of financial support that kept him from becoming a doctor. His other desire was to become a preacher or missionary. It is not surprising, then, that the information he gave from an unconscious state mirrored to an extent the desires he expressed about his life direction. Both come from a common source.

All of Cayce's early readings had to do with illness of the human body and what to do about it. When his directions were followed, the patient most often improved. There were some who asked for help when they were beyond recall with cancer or other serious diseases; Cayce would tell them that their pain could be eased but they could not be cured. Most of those asking for help, however, got it, and in ways that influenced the physiology of the body to return to normal.

In discussing concepts of healing the human body, Cayce emphasized the relationship among our spiritual, mental, and physical natures and the necessity of recognizing their unity in restoring health to the body. To fail to recognize this relationship is to miss the reality of what makes the difference between health and disease.

Contrary to this reality, the practice of medicine in recent years has become so mechanized in many specialties that the true source of healing—our God-given life force—has been neglected or simply forgotten. Perhaps it was never even recognized in the first place. When a patient looks at the doctor and says, "You can make me well," the physician is tempted to believe that he or she indeed is the one who is doing the healing. Whenever I, as a physician, am so tempted, I recall Cayce's words on the subject:

> Let those that minister know that all healing, all force and power comes from the Infinite; that those influences and powers that work in and through them, in making the application, can, will, through those promises He has given, manifest health, strength, vitality, for this body. (no. 735–4)*

Cayce said that medicines, compounds, and mechanical appliances all have their place as instruments of healing. The business of arousing hope, of creating confidence, of bringing faith into the consciousness of an individual is also very necessary.

> For who healeth all thy diseases? Only when any portion of the anatomical structure of a human being is put in accord with the divine influences, which is a portion of the consciousness of an individual entity, may real healing come. Without it, it is nil and becomes more destructive than constructive. (no. 5083–2)

As we near the end of the twentieth century, people throughout the world are learning that they have the power to choose. They are beginning to make choices, and in the process, are learning more about their own true nature—that they indeed are creatures of the Divine and have powers of healing within their own bodies that can not only help them to overcome a disease but can also maintain a healthy body, if used in the proper manner. These are patients who

---

*Each of the Edgar Cayce readings has been assigned a two-part number to provide easy reference. Each person who received a reading was given an anonymous number; this is the first half of the two-part number. Since many individuals obtained more than one reading, the second number designates the number of that reading in the series. Reading no. 735–4 was given for a person who was assigned case number 735. This particular reading was the fourth one he or she obtained from Cayce.

are seeking out the way and manner in which they would like to be treated. And they are beginning to recognize their own true nature.

In practicing as a family physician for forty years, my perspective on how health is created and how healing comes about has been changed tremendously by my experience with the material from the Edgar Cayce medical readings. Since 1955, both Gladys, my wife, and I have been working with the concepts from the readings in our medical practice.

Results have been occasionally disappointing, but mostly they have been either pleasing, surprising, or simply amazing. Our patients often respond in ways we had not anticipated, and healing comes about at times when it seems improbable or almost impossible.

Since 1970, when we launched the Association for Research and Enlightenment (A.R.E.) Clinic in Phoenix, we've enlarged the medical staff and expanded the variety of the therapeutic services that were suggested in the readings. Cayce recommended medical, osteopathic, and chiropractic care, and therapeutic massage and colonics were frequently advised. We have added electromagnetic field therapy, transcutaneous electrotherapy, and other forms of treatment that were only implied in the readings. For the past ten years, we have offered nine-day and seventeen-day residential programs that have brought together medical and therapeutic services designed to awaken in the patients a recognition of their true potential for full health.

My objective in this book is to share practical information that anyone can use to start or accelerate the healing process no matter what the ailment may be. Much of this practical information can be used at home, such as exercises, good nutrition, prayer, meditation, establishing new emotional habit patterns of response, and learning to recognize that one is truly of divine origin and destiny.

This is a book to be read for ideas and directions on how to improve your health and consciousness; it is written to urge you or your friends and loved ones onto the path of increased awareness toward your destiny in relationship to the Source. It is one doctor's observations and experiences in the field of healing, using the Edgar Cayce concepts of health as a primary guideline, superimposed on an educational foundation in conventional medicine and a degree and license to practice that profession.

Thus, it is directed primarily toward the general public, but also to the interested medical professional and scientist, for whatever ideas they may find stimulating. It carries with it respect for the spiritual nature of every human being and the knowledge and conviction that each of us here on this earthly plane has ultimate potential that we hardly dare dream of.

And, too, this book challenges each one who reads it to try the concepts that came out of the unconscious mind of this remarkable seer and to discover the joys of physical and mental health and soul growth that are everyone's destiny.

It is intended, then, to fulfill a deeply ingrained need for those who are seeking a path through life that we have come to call an "adventure in consciousness"—a path that Cayce suggested is really the work of the Christ in the earth today.

William A. McGarey, M.D.
Phoenix, Arizona

Energy Medicine
in the West

1

Medicine
Undergoing Change

*The physician should not treat the disease, but the patient
who is suffering from it.*

—MAIMONIDES

MEDICINE—SCIENTIFIC MEDICINE, ALLOPATHIC medicine*—
has lost its direction. At least, it has if some of the most revered figures
in medical history are to be given credit for knowing what medicine
is all about. It was eight hundred years ago that Maimonides put into
those few words quoted at the head of this chapter just what he
thought was the essence of the practice of medicine.

Maimonides was not alone in his directions to those who would
follow. Hippocrates once said, "There are in fact two things, science
and opinion; the former begets knowledge, the latter ignorance." Science has gathered much valuable information pertaining to the practice of medicine, and thus we *know* many things very well. Scientific
methods have made it possible to transplant vital organs, to detect

---

*A system of medical practice with remedies that produce effects different from those
of the disease treated.

3

accurately the sex of an unborn infant, to determine the extent of the spread of a cancer and the location and type of serious illnesses. We should value and follow the scientific method in that respect. But the world is filled with a multitude of realities that science has not tested, does not understand or even recognize. Some of these realities, when observed in the daily practice of medicine, are termed anecdotes and dismissed as insignificant. But they carry much wisdom, and they show sometimes just how far short scientific medicine is of the goal of understanding human beings.

A good example from my own practice is the case of four-year-old Beth, whose mother brought her to the A.R.E. Clinic as "a last resort." When Beth was two years old, she fell down the stairs at home. At the time she weighed twenty-three pounds, but for the next two years she gained no weight even though she continued to grow in height. She had the appearance of a starving child, and had been diagnosed by previous doctors who examined her as having a malabsorption syndrome and a megacolon; that is, her intestinal tract refused to absorb foods and her colon had become exceptionally large. Even though she ate almost continuously, she did not gain weight and she had a bowel movement only once every two weeks. Her arms and her legs looked like sticks, and she had difficulty—because of the pain it caused—even walking across the room. Her mother had been told that the prognosis was death by starvation. It was at that point that she decided to bring her daughter to our seventeen-day Temple Beautiful Program.

Beth, we soon discovered, was highly intelligent and very skilled at manipulating her mother through temper tantrums, which made it difficult to help her. In reviewing her medical history, we noted something that had been overlooked, or given no importance if it had been noted. When Beth fell, at the age of two, she landed flat on her "tummy." Our understanding of physiology told us that her fall probably shocked her solar plexus. That in turn had created an imbalance in her autonomic nervous system, that part of the nervous system that governs involuntary actions. This imbalance acted to produce failure of assimilation and the laxity of nerve supply that produced the megacolon. Her appetite was undiminished, but she could not use the food that she took into her body.

It was understandable that Beth was demanding. It hurt her to stand; and to walk across the room was almost impossible, it gave her so much pain. She had learned how to get her mother's attention—a temper tantrum would do this quite handily—so she called on that at will to get her mom to do things or even to carry her. Her mother could not tell when Beth was just manipulating her.

We helped Beth's mother out on this score, for it was not good for Beth to "use" her mom like that. Our staff was instructed how to respond to the tantrums. One day early in the program, Beth wanted something and didn't get it. Result: a tantrum! She lay on the floor, face down, kicking her feet and screaming, until suddenly her voice changed and she began crying.

Her mother knew she had hurt her foot, lying there and kicking, so she ran over and picked the little girl up and comforted her. As she was in her mother's arms, being quieted, Beth sobbed through her tears, "Why do I do this to myself?" Not many adults would come up with that kind of self-observation.

Beth was put on a special diet filled with greens and fresh food, fish and fowl, soups and good bread. She started to flourish. She received vitamin and enzyme supplements, castor oil packs across her abdomen, a dropperful of castor oil on her tongue at bedtime, full-body massages, and electromagnetic field therapy. She also learned something about biofeedback techniques and exercises to do with her mother.

She was taught relaxation techniques, visualization, and autogenics associated with biofeedback training. We worked with her in her dream imagery, and through the use of hand puppets, Beth learned how to release anger.

On the spiritual level, Beth progressed from an attitude of self-centeredness to one of helping others. She was the focal point of healing prayer, laying on of hands, loving care, and consistent positive reinforcement. She learned to relate to other program participants and staff in a positive manner.

At the end of the seventeen-day program, she had gained three pounds, whereas her weight gain in the two years prior had been zero. When asked just before the program ended in September how long it would take to make her well, she replied, "Six weeks!"

It was a self-fulfilled prophecy. The next January she was one of the case presentations at our annual medical symposium. She was running around, acting like any other four-and-a-half-year-old healthy girl who is filled with vibrant life.

Three years later I received this note: "I am the grandfather of the four-year-old girl that came to your clinic for help, and you opened up your heart and gave us life. I would call it a miracle."

Of course it was not a miracle but simply recognizing that the physiology of the body had been disturbed in a significant way by an injury, and that there are ways of correcting that malfunction.

As this is being written, Beth is ten years old and fulfilling some of the tremendous potential that all of us at the Clinic recognized during her stay here.

"Wisdom is knowing what to do next. Skill is knowing how to do it. Virtue is doing it!" This is an old bit of truth, certainly, but the unknown author must have tuned in to the same source that Edgar Cayce located when he said to take what you have in hand and begin!

Beth's success story would fail to impress medical science, because such reports of single events "are condescendingly called anecdotes: stories concocted by well-meaning but scientifically naive clinicians," notes Dr. Richard V. Lee. In his paper "The Singular Sadness of Numerical Madness" (*Continuing Education*, September 1983), Dr. Lee points out that numbers and statistics have taken the place of the

careful attention to the individual and the commonplace, previously the hallmark of the excellent clinician. How many important and interesting biological events go unnoticed by blinkered academicians working single-mindedly at collecting series of patients or diseases big enough to publish?

Contemporary medicine shares with the culture that shapes it a steady decline in appreciation and respect for the individual and the unique. One test, one patient, one problem cannot begin to satisfy the voracious appetite statistically significant doctors have for multitudes of numbers and crowds of patients. . . For the best possible outcome, each patient needs, has a right to expect, her/his doctor's undivided attention and effort. To judge the patient, the illness, and the medical effort only by averages and percentages demeans both the patient and doctor and diminishes the importance of illness. . . . The essence of medicine, as opposed to public health, statistics, and politics, remains the communion of a patient with a physician: an intensive examination of the complaints and the biology of one person by one physician. Sadly, this special one-to-one relationship is in danger of becoming just another statistic.

Dr. Lee's observations serve to confirm that medicine has indeed lost its direction. How did it happen? At one time medicine to a great extent was taught only through the preceptor approach. The doctor in practice took on a young student who wanted to learn how to be a doctor; this was a major portion of the young doctor's education, and medical schools were not associated with universities. Early in this century, the universities took on the teaching of medical students, and the professors supplemented their income by doing research—mostly for drug companies. The direction of medical education then turned away from the human being and toward the correction of a disease.

It is very difficult to do a double-blind statistical study on someone like Beth; or on the innermost physiological balances within the body, which cannot be accurately measured in their actions but only by their effects on the body as a whole. It is much easier to study diseases, because one can see that fifty instances of streptococcus sore throat repond better to one drug than to another.

When doctors aim toward the study of disease, the human being who is the creator of the disease gets lost in the shuffle. It is like having to choose between two completely different destinations. We choose one direction knowing that in the process we must give up the other destination.

Thus, as the disease becomes the prime object of so-called scientific study, the one-on-one relationship between patient and physician is eventually forgotten. As diseases become the gods of medicine, the diagnosis becomes the gathering of food for the gods.

The patient—the human being who comes into the office of any physician licensed to practice medicine—is a wonderful, amazing accumulation of activities that we call physiological functions. But more than that, much more, the patient is a manifestation of a life force, a consciousness that directs whether one is healthy or ill, whether there is adequate acid in the stomach or too much, whether the heart beats too rapidly or just fast enough for the activity being encountered. This life force is what the Chinese call the *chi*. We in the Western world recognize it as the electricity flowing through the nervous system and through the other tissues of the body that makes it a living body. Without this life force, life would not exist.

The stresses that one encounters in life create turmoil in the physical body by upsetting the normal flow of electricity—whereas peace or laughter or forgetting oneself in service create a more coherent flow of electricity that strengthens the life forces.

Increasingly, the scientific approach of medicine has taken the nation's doctors deeply into the pathology of disease while whisking them away from the individual patient's fears, difficulties, and general life situation, as if these had nothing to do with the origin or worsening of a disease. In a study conducted in 1977 of 11,053 patients in Veterans Administration hospitals, 85 percent said that their physicians were thorough and competent, but only 35 percent felt that their doctors listened to them adequately or spent enough time with them.

Every basic study in medicine leads one to diseases, which are processes that involve the patient's life-style, environment, feelings and emotions, beliefs, stresses, and more significantly, his or her immune system.

Fortunately there are those, outside of medicine and within, who are helping to change its direction. For example, Joseph A. Califano, Jr., Secretary of Health, Education, and Welfare under President Carter, wrote in the preface to the 1979 report "Healthy People: The Surgeon General's Report on Health Promotion and Disease Prevention," "Let us make no mistake about the significance of this document. It represents an emerging consensus among scientists and the health community that the nation's health strategy must be dramatically recast to emphasize the prevention of disease."

Califano's words have not yet made a tremendous change in promoting health, but they must be considered a significant move, pointing the way for the field of medicine. His observations did not point directly to the physiology of the body as a major factor in the process, but the inference is there.

Dr. Herbert Benson, reporting on the early effects of medical and surgical therapies in the June 1979 *New England Journal of Medicine*, concluded that much relief that far exceeded what could be expected from the treatments alone was due to positive thinking, physician-patient rapport, and the patients' belief that what they were getting was beneficial. Benson later noted that we've developed such faith in science that we feel medicines do it on their own. Medicines cannot, of course, act in that manner. We can aid any potent medication by paying attention to the basics of a doctor-patient relationship. It enhances any therapy and in some cases even makes the therapy.

What emerged from the study, perhaps, was the recognition of the value of the patient's belief or faith. What was not explored or suggested were the physiological pathways or the mind-effect or the visualization power that allowed the patient's belief to be effective in the physical body. The Edgar Cayce readings suggest that one might know what a therapy does in one's conscious mind, then *see* it happen in the body. There is also the effect on the immune system of a positive outlook. A positive attitude tips the acid-alkaline balance in the tissues of the body toward the alkaline side, which in turn allows the lymphocytes and the lymphatic vessels and their contents to function more efficiently. Perhaps the effect is generated by a healthier adrenal gland, which is enhanced by laughter or a brightened attitude.

For decades doctors have believed that the disease or symptoms can be treated with medicine or surgery without recognizing that the physiology of the body, the emotions, the conscious and unconscious mind, and the spiritual nature of the human being are also deeply involved in the process. Such a concept must be changed if the nature of the human body is ever to be understood by those who offer help to the ailing.

The medical profession must eventually face up to its purpose and the truths that lie behind that purpose. As physicians, we are given the responsibility of caring for the health and welfare of those who become ill. More importantly, we must know the human being well enough to help prevent illnesses from occurring as much as possible. Behind that purpose lies the desire to be of service, to give something valuable to humanity. The desire and the purpose are intertwined in daily living, and they influence both medical doctors and students in training.

Cayce saw the basic need of any human being to be of service. His concept of treating the whole person involved the recognition that we are body, mind, and spirit. If any one part of this triune is left unattended, then neither the treatment—nor the understanding—is complete. We are essentially spiritual beings, with creative minds and bodies that are fashioned as a result of that spirit in action.

The essence of Cayce's philosophy has been expressed by others, such as Felix Marti-Ibañez, who was probably the most respected medical writer of his day. He was admired perhaps because he said or wrote what all doctors deep in their hearts wanted to hear and yet were unable to really practice. He had, in any event, much that was worthwhile to say. In an essay for *M.D. Magazine* in November 1960, he dealt with what all physicians need to hold high in their minds, in their acts, and in their teachings.

> Every day, more and more, medicine becomes, above all, the prevention of disease and the promotion of health. For only by knowing the healthy man can we cure him when he falls ill. Knowledge of the healthy man is obtained by studying our fellow beings, both the healthy and the diseased, not only in the mirror of classical and modern medical literature but also in current newspapers.
>
> . . . The physician in his threefold capacity, as a professional, as a member of society, and as a human being, has throughout history helped man in his physical, mental, and social ascent. As a professional man in particular, the physician has always acted as a healer, using magic, faith, empiricism, or rational resources; as a knower, for he knows the secrets of nature and of the human being; as a preventer, for he can arrest disease by forestalling its inroads before they develop; and as an organizer, for he can guide society in fighting the historicosocial process called disease. To heal, to know, to prevent, to organize—these

will be your four future spheres of professional activity, embraced in the expression "to be a doctor."

To be a doctor, then, means much more than to dispense pills or to patch up or repair torn flesh and shattered minds. To be a doctor is to be an intermediary between man and God.

To hear what Marti-Ibañez had to say is one thing. To practice it is another. If the medical profession is to change, it will probably not come from within. Most physicians are too busy with their own duties to spend time seeking out the need for change and making it happen. The medical schools have created such strong thought-forms that the professors (for the most part) adopt the thought-forms and continue teaching in the way their predecessors have taught. And there is little place in the medical school curriculum for the idea of a Supreme Being.

The change may come about more simply than one would suspect. It will take the patient population demanding to be part of the healing experience, demanding that their doctors recognize them as body, mind, and spirit, demanding that doctors recognize that all healing in reality comes from within, that treatments from outside can only aid in bringing that attunement which allows the cells and the organs to recognize their divinity and return to a normal state, demanding that their doctors recognize that health is the goal the body is trying to accomplish all the time and that assistance can be given creatively to realize such a goal.

The more these demands are made, the more doctors will change. Unless it does come about in that manner, the change is likely to be very, very slow.

2

The Cayce Viewpoint on Health and Disease

Have you ever wondered just what kind of creature you are? All through my life, in my studies through college and medical school and in my church, I've wondered about my own real nature. I find that I can think, I can imagine, I can speak, I can laugh and cry. The animals around me cannot do these things, yet God made them, too, I am told. Why do we, then, have these capacities? Why are we, above all God's creatures, gifted to create music and sculpture, stories and poetry?

Upon finishing my medical training and starting the practice of medicine, I still did not have satisfactory answers. But later, in studying the Cayce readings, I came across information that seemed to elaborate on what I've been able to grasp from the Bible—my primary source for understanding the nature of God.

> In the beginning, when there was the creating, or the calling of individual entities into being, we were made to be the companions with the Father-God. (no. 1567–2)

The exquisite nature of the human odyssey as we prepare to become companions of God is revealed, rather poetically, in this reading:

Know that life is as a river or a stream which is constant, and each appearance is as a pool that may refresh, in which others may be refreshed, or become stagnant and not get very far in a development in a material or earthly sojourn; or it may apply the truths of the spirit—as the ripple, as the roar of the cataract, as a part of thy physical consciousness in every experience. Use the power thus generated—not to self-indulgence but to beautify, to make the world a better place because you have lived in it. You can only do that by the hour, by the moment, by the day you live. (no. 5392–1)

Is it any wonder that God provided the miraculous process of healing of this wonderful creation? To understand the healing process we must see ourselves as a body-mind-spirit entity. There is a oneness that encompasses all three. There is an energy that connects all three—the life force. But more than that, we should look at ourselves as an ongoing stream of consciousness, a creation that is constantly changing even as we think about it, a being shaped by experiences, both constructive and destructive, in this life and in many past lives.

Healing needs to be seen as a process of attuning ourselves, our energies, to our true nature, that of becoming companions, cocreators with the Father-God. Less than that would be less than adequate. The attuning comes in many forms, touching the physical body, the mental, and the spiritual.

To gain a perspective from Cayce's standpoint, it helps to go directly to that source and see what he means by identifying us as physical, mental, and spiritual beings in need of healing. The following excerpt is a long one, but important:

. . . the body finds self in a material world; with a physical body subject to all the laws and the rules and the regulations, not only of the material desires, needs or necessities, but that which has been created by the attitude of the body towards things, conditions, circumstances of a spiritual and mental *and* a material nature. . . .

Then, in the physical being, we find there are those conditions that are of the physical nature that have become subject to the purely material influences through the allowing of the creating of poisons through the system, through the poor assimilation, poor elimination. . . .

So, as the mind is the builder with those things that are of hate, dislikes, grudges, selfishness, dirty and dark, dingy things that are a portion of every experience—and not with the sunlight of happiness, joy, hopefulness, patience, brotherly love; it, too, becomes besmirched and subject to those things to which it, the mind, becomes enslaved. . . .

Then, because there may be used those physical attributes that might or may or will be a helpful influence to rid the body of the physical disturbances, do not consider that these are going without the veil of spirituality or of mental science, or of mental cleanliness.

For how does one cleanse the mind? By the pouring out, the forgetting, the laying aside of those things that easily beset and *filling* same with pure, fresh water that is of the eternal life, that is of the eternal goodness as may be found in Him who *is* the light, the way, the truth, the vine, the bread of life and the water of life. These things are those influences that purify.

Then the motivative element may be within the attributes of nature itself, whether it be through mechanical applications or medicinal properties or herbs. *Whose* herbs are they? Whose force or power is used? They are *One!*

Then, wherein does the mind function? To use that thou hast in hand! What need is there for a better body, save to serve thy fellow man the better? For he that is the greatest among you is the servant of all. This is not only referring to those who teach, to those who minister, to those who wait on this, that or the other influence, but to each and every soul—and to every phase of the soul's activity in a material world! (no. 1620–1)

Healing must be thought of, then, as a combination of the cleansing of the body, the purifying of the mind, and an attuning with the creative forces of the universe. It is not just taking a shot of penicillin, or having a spinal adjustment or a massage, or experiencing the laying on of hands in prayer, or going through a visualization experience. Healing, most of the time, is not just applying one mode of treatment. It's an experience in the ongoing stream of life, which Cayce likened to a pool that may refresh or be a means of applying the truths of the spirit.

Some years ago we were in telephone communication with a

young couple whose infant son developed apnea, periods of time when he momentarily stopped breathing, frightening those who observed the episode. The parents certainly were frightened, for time after time, they were forced to call for an ambulance and take the child to the emergency room.

The parents were told to speak to the child as an equal, especially when they put him to bed, and tell him they loved him, wanted him to stay with them. At the Clinic, the nurse they contacted recommended that they pray long and hard and massage him alongside the spine, using peanut oil. The parents followed the regimen diligently, calling frequently for support, and the number of episodes decreased from two to four times daily to just three or four a week. This improvement took only two weeks.

By the time the child was six months old, the episodes occurred once a week or less frequently. Before he was a year old, they had stopped. The child, the parents—all three—have had a major life experience. What did they learn? That there are ways of working with a physical body and its physiology to bring about health once again, even when a good therapy for an illness is not really available.

Many years ago, Edgar Cayce gave a reading for another couple who wanted to heal, one by the laying on of hands and the other using "energies in nature itself." They were given some guidance in a reading:

> Then unifying these, let both in their own method, in their own manner apply same; yet knowing deep within self that the *source* of power, the *source* of might, the *source* of grace, the *source* of mercy, the *source* of life, the *source* of health comes only from the *living* God. (no. 688–4)

Their reading reminded me of the mother and father using not only massage, which is the laying on of hands in a sense, but also peanut oil, which is "energy in nature itself." And it gives us additional insight into the process and the source of what we call healing.

In medical school, we study anatomy, physiology, and biochemistry to aid us in understanding the body, so that we might treat it more adequately. We learn about the structures that together make up the entire physical body, the way in which the internal organs and systems function, and the chemical reactions that occur all the time as the body continues living.

We also study pathology, a course that gives most medical students the greatest difficulty. Pathology shows us what tissue looks like when it is diseased, not when it is healthy. In dead tissue that has been preserved so it can be seen through the microscope, it is difficult to see what makes life exist. Pathology, of course, is more than just that, but the direction of that particular science is not to determine what health is, but rather how to diagnose a disease by what has happened to the tissue.

Looking at the human being from the standpoint of concepts in the Cayce readings, I find counterparts to those that I studied in medical school. Anatomy, for instance, is much the same in many respects, except that Cayce adds something: we are first and foremost an energy being, created in the image of that Creative Power we call God. God is what we call Spirit. God is also love, which complicates the picture a lot, if one really deals with that concept, for it means that the spirit which is life itself within our being is also love. This power then is either hidden from view deep inside us or manifested in our external relationships with others. Our physical body—that three-dimensional reality we call physical—is really composed of atoms thrown together, in a sense, to form molecules and other biochemical, structural units, then cells, organs, systems, and whatever else is needed to fill out the energy pattern that is our own reality. This is the reality our bodies manifest through the many incarnations we experience on the earthly plane.

This is true of nature, also, for the earth and all it contains is also made up of atoms. We have a Catalina pine tree in our front yard. It was about three feet high when we planted it. Unfortunately, the trunk of the tree was broken off in an accident shortly after it was planted. We saw that the tree continued to live, so we watched it. The branches, winding in a circle around the base of the broken-off trunk, were beautiful, so we didn't disturb things. In the next three years, one of the branches took it upon itself to meet the needs of the whole tree to *grow*, and it changed. Gradually, the tip of the branch curved over toward the center of the tree where the trunk had been, and it became larger in diameter than the other branches. It even grew new branches out of its own newly designed branch-trunk. It took over the function of the trunk that had been destroyed, so that the energy pattern of the tree itself could be fulfilled. Now, with the new trunk in the centerline of the tree, it is over four feet tall, and the curve is almost straightened out.

We see similar results in the human being where a portion is destroyed or damaged and regeneration occurs to fulfill the destiny of the energy body of the human being—more about that later on.

Let's look at physiology. In medicine, this discipline assumes that physiological functioning for the most part is basically biochemical. Even neurological impulses are brought about through biochemical means. A new, more rational concept has been growing in medical research. It aligns itself unknowingly with the concepts that were verbalized by Edgar Cayce during the first half of this century. Those ideas have been around that long and longer.

Cayce indicated that every cell, every organ, every system, and even every atom of the human body has consciousness. The concept that an atom might have consciousness is difficult to understand and accept. Of course, once it is accepted by faith or proved by research, the cell, the organ systems, and thus the entire body must be recognized as having the same physiological nature.

In medical research, it seems that consciousness is being dealt with in the laboratories, although it is not given that name. It appears in the study of viruses and bacteria. The medical writer Julian DeVries, writing about the growth and activity of viruses and bacteria in *Arizona Republic* (March 29, 1976), said that these

> microscopic biochemical components . . . constantly are at war between themselves and their external and internal environment. Like the humans of which they are integral parts, they form and break alliances with each other. Some, following the pattern of international intrigue, act as double agents, scientists report. In this never-ending battle, evolutionary changes constantly take place which enable the microscopic participants either to play more effective roles, or to become the slaves of more dominant factions, or even to be absorbed and become a part of them.

Just like us humans, aren't they? They are either moving upward on the scale of consciousness and growth toward their destiny, or down toward dissolution and loss of identity.

Perhaps the problem with medicine lies in the solution being sought. Instead of dealing with consciousness, medical research seeks pharmacological means to stop, prevent, or reverse biological events involving these bacteria or viruses. Isn't that what we do in human affairs? Instead of promoting the awareness that humanity should become one in consciousness with the Creative Force that brought us all into being, we conquer countries to stop them from leading the kind of life they choose to lead, we kill to bring peace, and we prevent further destruction by creating massive instruments of destruction.

The new consciousness coming about in the basic study of the human being alters the old biochemical basis of physiological activity in the body. Thought and electrical impulses or electromagnetic fields induce action, utilizing the body's biochemical mechanisms to make it happen—so energy comes first, the way life comes first. And much as in the human body and its formation, function comes first, structure next.

In the Cayce readings, physiology is a process that must be coordinated in order for the body to enjoy good health. It is much like a group working in a factory. They must work together in order to bring about the best results. If one worker is ill or loafs on the job, there comes about an uncoordinant activity, which spells eventual trouble.

In the body, it's much the same. The liver must coordinate its activities properly with the kidney or the eliminations are faulty, and the body becomes ill at ease, experiences dis-ease. In one of his readings, Cayce enumerated seven different incoordinations in the body of the person for whom he was giving a reading.

If, for instance, after a lower back injury, the sacral parasympathetic plexus (a group of nerves lying deep in the pelvis) puts out faulty messages through its part of the autonomic nervous system, and the prostate malfunctions and develops into what is called prostatic hypertrophy (an enlargement of the prostate), then there are certain consequences. The nerves coming from the prostate send their distress signals to the autonomic, the cerebrospinal nervous system gets involved (at least to an extent), and secondary symptoms can arise directly from the malfunctioning prostate. Perhaps there would be an upper abdominal reaction creating excess acid in the stomach. This would be termed hyperacidity of the stomach, or, if it progresses far enough, an ulcer. All because the sacral parasympathetic plexus put out messages that were faulty. It's interesting how complicated we can really get in creating our own diseases, isn't it?

Numerous other examples could be cited, but the important thing is to recognize that each organ, each system of the body must function in a cooperative manner with the other organs and systems in order to bring about a state of good health. This is the physiology of the Cayce material. And to bring about a return of the normal, coordinated function is to restore good, abundant health.

Recently, I was visiting a friend whose son was having a real problem with allergies and difficult breathing. He had taken some medicines the night before but had not done well. He hadn't been to school that day, and in the meantime, he developed a fever.

It happened that I knew that the diet Joe followed was not good and that there was considerable tension in the home at times. His diet and the stress of emotional tension created an overacidity in the body and symptoms of sore throat and allergy, fever, and the like. I suggested that his mother give Joe lots of water, juices, and some clear, hot soup if he desired and, to quiet his body down, use a castor oil pack on his abdomen and another one around his neck for the sore throat. I suggested also that he take one Alka Seltzer in water about every eight hours and continue the vitamins he was already using.

The next morning, Joe was well, up and hungry, off to school, acting as if he had never been sick. The overacid condition in his tissues had been corrected. It seems that with the increased acidity, the immune system was depressed temporarily. After it was corrected, the body itself took care of the bacteria that had invaded the throat.

Increased acidity in the tissues is one level of etiology (causation). It does not deal, however, with the underlying causes, about which I have only sketchy information in Joe's case. But it shows what often predisposes a body to illness, and how to restore, in many cases, a state of health, or at least, homeostasis (internal equilibrium). Any system, especially the physiological system of higher animals, tends to maintain internal stability, coordinating the response of its parts to any stimulation disturbing its normal condition or function.

In trying to understand how we go about creating either health or disease, and taking into consideration my belief that God did create each human being on this globe, and that he did it with love and *is* love, I gradually developed a concept that explains to my satisfaction most instances of health or lack of it in the human being. Later in this chapter and those that follow, we will explore the steps that lead ultimately to health or disease. But for now we ask, Why?

Why did Joe move from the state of health to dis-ease, then to disease? The disease was infectious pharyngitis, an allergic syndrome. It could be called that. Approaching the question from the standpoint of function, it can be understood that the immune system (the thymus and lymphatic system) and the upper part of the respiratory tree both became functionally deficient. Most likely Joe's assimilation and elimination functions were not working correctly, probably partly due to his diet, which is really part of his external environment.

It could be simply his life-style—his habit, perhaps, of going to bed too late and not getting enough sleep, an exercise program that was not health-producing, and a diet that contained too many starches, sugars, colas, candy, and desserts, and was too acid-reacting (creating a lower pH in blood and/or body tissues) in its nature. His heredity, on the other hand, may have influenced his respiratory tree or his immune system to be more sensitive to foods and the external world. Or it could be influences from emotions and attitudes built up in prior lives that currently are part of his unconscious mind, affecting the endocrine glands and the hormones and neurological impulses arising there. An imbalance, for instance, in the seven spiritual centers and their associated glandular structures would bring about an imbalance in those life functions and the life-support systems and organs.

Disturbance in his home that he could not readily deal with emotionally might be the answer, or he might have been rebelling against something confronting him at the time.

All this takes one back to the reality that each person is in the three-dimensional plane—the earth—with a conscious mind that has the power of choosing from moment to moment how to act, how to believe, how to respond emotionally, and how to change or hold on to one's attitudes. Joe chose to use my suggestions to move toward health.

Being created in the image of God means that we are really souls in the earth, in an energy body that we have had from the very beginning. It means also that we have been given the abilities that God has, so we can be cocreators with him. A tremendous challenge! As souls, we are mind (which is the builder), spirit (which is the life), and will (which gives us the power to choose). The choice is the real key to change, and the change that comes about as one moves from disease to health is powered by the spirit of life that flows through each one of us and is directed by the mind choosing to go in a particular direction.

What's needed next is action. This is why Cayce so often said that it's better to do something "wrong" than to do nothing at all. In a sense, it doesn't matter whether we are going forward or backward—the important thing is to move! I think this would imply that action sooner or later will take us in the right direction, even though we may insist on going in the wrong direction until we have no place else to go but upward. Action, then, while we are in the earth, leads us eventually toward understanding and advancement. To choose in the right direction is to exercise that power and to move us closer to our eventual destiny.

We have used our choices in creating emotional patterns (habits) in past incarnations or sojourns in the earth. And they, in turn, have become part of our unconscious mind, probably locked in those seven spiritual centers but always available as an emotional reaction to a life situation that we might encounter this time around. If we are careful, we can watch those responses and see what we have indeed built. And, also, if we watch carefully, we can build new habit patterns of response in the present, thus altering the content of the unconscious as well as those patterns that are locked in the spiritual centers.

The conscious mind is the actor, the unconscious mind the reactor. We have the power in our conscious mind at the present time to change whatever we wish—but we need to work on the hidden patterns of response while we become active in this earthly plane doing those things that are constructive and not destructive. That's like using the power of choice to plant diamonds in our own backyard for later retrieval.

It's only as we build those positive emotional, attitudinal, and belief patterns in the unconscious mind that our present direction, our conscious choices and actions, become less in conflict with our "tendencies," those influences we have built into our unconscious over the many sojourns in the earth. For gradually, those "tendencies" become less and less present and apparent as they are replaced with a new program.

All these activities, choices, sojourns, influences, and so on play a part in creating in these wonderful bodies of ours a condition of health, dis-ease or disease. And it is always a process.

The process, of course, is designed in part by what we may call astral influences. These involve the experiences one has between incarnations, the teaching, the mental activities that occur in what we call the spiritual environment or the astral plane. In the Cayce readings, the implication is that we enter a new incarnation from one of the planets of this solar system, after receiving the kinds of mental teachings that go on there. This is difficult to understand, perhaps, but Cayce suggests that our astrological sign is tied up with that sort of activity. The needs of our soul level may be met by this kind of university setting, and I would suspect that there are higher powers that design the kind of teaching we may be subjected to at that level of the astral plane.

Cayce said that we do select the family we are born into; that's a choice made prior to being born. There are certain strengths and weaknesses found in that genetic strain that we need to manifest, and certain past-life experiences that we need to come in contact with that would be found in the two people who become our parents. There are friends to be met again in the life experience that we choose when we select our heredity, and perhaps also enemies, so heredity is more a matter of choice than we suspect.

The external environment might involve the smog we live in at the present time, the electrical and/or electromagnetic influences that surround us, the house we live in, the climate that becomes part of our life experience, the emotional situations that surround us, and perhaps a number of other factors that can or do alter our health. But we *do* choose whom we marry, where we will live, and the friends who become part of our lives. Thus we might blame external factors for causing an illness, but we have chosen to get into those environments.

The same can be said of our life-style. This is more commonly accepted as being changeable, as being under the control of one's choices. We do directly choose what we eat (even though our bodies most of the time override our better judgment). We exercise or not, according to what we have chosen to do, and we rest sufficiently, achieve balance in our lives through rest, recreation, work, and habits according to what we choose to do. These can all be changed by activating that gift of the Creator that we call will or choice.

In the same manner, the balance of the interactions of the seven spiritual centers comes about at least partially through choices made and actions taken. Emotions and attitudes find their home in these centers of energy, and the total influence emerging out of these areas is, in a sense, a coordinated single influence that is much like what we understand as a personality or an individuality. Seeing the manner in which all these centers relate with each other, it becomes more understandable why we respond emotionally in a manner that says, "This is just the way I am." It really affects each of us in that way. And it seems to be the truth.

This may be why we need a standard to look to, so we can find out if the "way we are" measures up to what, in our better moments, we really want to be. We call this standard an ideal. It is best recognized by admitting first that we really are spiritual beings, and then understanding as best we can what God is like. For we were created "in the image of God" (Gen. 1:27). God is best understood as love: "He that loveth not knoweth not God; for God is love" (1 John 4:8).

So this gives us an insight into the standard or ideal for each of us. Whatever is understood in the Bible as a definition of love might then be called our ideal. For me, the fruits of the spirit, which Paul described in Galatians (fifth chapter), meant the manner in which we can manifest the nature of God and thus move in a direction that takes us toward our eventual goal, oneness with God.

There is one significant influence that we have not yet discussed: the effect of God's help in our making of choices. It can be felt at any level, but his choices would not go contrary to ours or we would not really have free choice. And that gift was given us when we were created.

All of these influences have an effect and create a kind of homeostasis from their interactions. They in turn bring about in our bodies either what we would call health or a state of dis-ease or uneasiness or imbalance—which, if continued long enough, creates disease.

To treat the whole person adequately, then, it becomes obvious that first the nature of human beings must be understood, the reality of past-life experiences recognized, the power that lies inherent in the human frame gratefully acknowledged and the proper balance and coordination and functioning of the life-support systems and organs of the human body sought; and the guiding light must be the fact that disease of the human frame is always a process that can be reversed.

3

Miracles from Body Energies

WHILE ATTENDING THE FIRST International Conference on Energy Medicine held at Madras, India, in 1987, I recognized that energy medicine, at least its theoretical aspect, had come into its own. For the conference had brought together scientists and medical practitioners from East and West—from China, from the Soviet Union, from Europe and the United States—all of whom had one thing in common: a passionate belief in the healing potential of the mysterious electrical forces found in every human being. Most of those who attended are engaged in researching the part that energies play in healing. Drs. Sarada Subrahmanyam and T. M. Srinivasan, founders of the Madras Institute of Magnetobiology, which hosted the conference, called energy medicine the "science of tomorrow." If I were to disagree with them at all it would be to suggest that energy medicine won't wait until tomorrow. It is a medical concept whose time has come.

When we established an Energy Medicine Department at the A.R.E. Clinic in 1984, it seemed like a pioneering step, for few people were acquainted with this approach to healing. But the concept has caught the attention of many people during recent years, a period when we have all been looking for better answers to the health problems that plague the human race.

What is energy medicine? Paul Rosch, M.D., writing in *Medical Tribune* (March 25, 1987), said that it is involves working with a previously unappreciated or unrecognized universe of electrical activity in the human body: "Essentially this consists of the biological equivalent of electrical currents, which are switched on and off by injury, infection, malignancy, and certain normal activities."

Since doctors had not been aware of this electrical flow, they had no way of knowing that a healthy body requires the free movement of this form of energy. We may be no further along in understanding how it works than doctors were only a few generations ago when leeches were used because we thought sick people suffered from "bad blood." In any case, we still have much to learn about how it works. Dr. Rosch says, "Low-level electrical energies apparently are conducted through blood vessels and across capillary walls, causing white cells and metabolic compounds to migrate into and out of surrounding tissues. Such activities may be as important in preserving homeostatis as the circulation of the blood itself."

Though this seems like a revolutionary idea, some doctors began working with electrical therapies as early as the turn of the century. In 1905 Clarence Edward Skinner, M.D., wrote in *Therapeutics of Dry Hot Air* (New York: A. L. Chatterton, 1902) about "the so-called 'physiological' forces: heat, cold, electricity, the various forms of radiant energy, etc." as "new forces" in the therapeutic world that he thought were destined "to revolutionize the current methods of treating many disease processes." Dr. Skinner was quite right, only it has taken longer than he predicted. The medical profession tended to ignore those "new forces" in favor of altering the body chemistry to combat disease. Thus most physicians in our time have been trained to combat illness with an array of chemicals in the form of easy-to-take capsules.

Colleagues in the chiropractic field, of course, differed. They have been telling us for years that the body's electrical circuits are critical to the state of our health. When they manipulate the spine to make sure that each vertebra is properly aligned, one of their objectives is to make sure the electrical circuits are clear to all our organs from the brain through the spinal column. A misaligned vertebra can cause much more than a pain in your back; it can block the energy flow to one or more of your vital organs that require it to function efficiently. Patients in our programs at the Clinic routinely receive chiropractic examinations. Spinal adjustments are one form of energy medicine.

But for the medical profession, drugs became the preferred solution. Patients came to believe that the "right" drug would surely heal them. The fact is, of course, that the only function various drugs can perform is to change the body chemistry, to kill or render helpless certain bacteria or viruses, and to force various physiological functions. The doctor who prescribes these drugs hopes that the change will help the body to overcome the problem—to heal itself. And this can bring healing, if the change in consciousness within comes about. Body chemistry and physiology are both very complex, however, and unexpected side effects bid us all to caution when using drugs.

In recent years there has been increasing interest among physicians and patients in alternative means of restoring health to the body. Addictions to drugs, both the legal prescription variety and illegal substances, has become so widespread that hardly a family exists that has not suffered the consequences in some way. The rampant problem of drug abuse has spurred the quest for sensible alternatives.

Since the late 1960s a growing number of doctors have recognized that the medical profession must explore other pathways to health. Doctors themselves must not remain "hooked" on prescribing drugs. They must learn more about such basics as diet and nutrition. They must recognize the interplay between emotional disturbances and physical ills. They must expand their awareness and look at the patient as a whole—body, mind, and spirit—and not just as a case of this disease or that. They must become more skilled in treating the whole person, get at the root of the problem and not just treat the disease or its symptoms.

The movement toward a new age of health care within the medical profession has been slow but steadily gaining momentum. It has surfaced through the formation of several organizations since the 1970s, notably the American Holistic Medical Association. Its first president, Norman Shealy, a neurosurgeon from Wisconsin, typifies the expanding consciousness of medical practitioners, for Dr. Shealy gave up surgery in favor of holistic therapies that he regards as a better way. He has also lectured and written many articles on the subject, including his regular column in *New Realities* magazine, as a way of educating the public to expect and request this kind of health care.

Another breakthrough organizational effort worth noting is that of the Academy of Parapsychology and Medicine, which a number of us formed in 1970 to conduct instructional conferences for doctors interested in becoming acquainted with alternative methods of facilitating the healing process. The Academy's meetings covered everything from acupuncture to psychic surgery, from prayer to laying on of hands. As a barometer of the interest in such new therapies, one conference held at Stanford University drew three thousand physicians. The Academy had a short life (for financial reasons) but a significant one during a time of change.

The Menninger Research Foundation in Kansas during this same period launched an invitational conference on biofeedback at the instigation of Elmer Green, a specialist in that innovative field. The conference, held at Council Grove, Kansas, has become an annual affair devoted really to consciousness change throughout the world.

The Medical Symposium that my wife, Gladys, and I sponsored in 1968 before we formed the A.R.E. Clinic explored Cayce's approach to medicine and has become a very popular annual event, attracting researchers from many fields.

Popular interest in Edgar Cayce's concepts blossomed during this same period as a result of Jess Stearn's best-seller *Edgar Cayce: The Sleeping Prophet*, which led to many other books on specific Cayce topics such as dreams, reincarnation, and meditation. Milton Friedman, a former speechwriter for President Ford who was one of our speakers at the Medical Symposium in 1978, talked about official

Washington's growing interest in meditation, prayer, and dream study. "The ghost of Edgar Cayce stalks the streets and halls of Washington, and a new consciousness has taken hold among lawmakers. The cutting edge of the New Consciousness seems to be in the area of health," Friedman said, "and it's a heightened knowledge about what makes someone sick, and an awareness that this knowledge applied is more important than fixing up the body when something goes wrong."

The impact of Cayce, controversial as he may have been among skeptics, was so great that even the editor of the *Journal of the American Medical Association*, John P. Callan, M.D., paid tribute to him as the father of holistic medicine. In a thoughtful editorial in the March 1975 issue, Dr. Callan recognized that holistic medicine was no passing fad but an approach that the medical profession needed to take seriously. Holistic practitioners treat the whole person, not simply diseases, Callan pointed out, and their practitioners profess that Western, scientific medicine is too disease oriented and splits mind from body. Callan suggested that the supporters of holism plan to make their brand of medicine a top national priority, and recommended that physicians learn more about it. He found holism closely related to the work of the Association for Research and Enlightenment in Virginia Beach, Virginia:

> The roots of present-day holism probably go back 100 years to the birth of Edgar Cayce in Hopkinsville, KY. By the time he died in 1945, Cayce was well recognized as a mystic who entered sleep trances and dictated a philosophy of life and healing called "readings." His base was established at Virginia Beach, VA, now the headquarters of the Cayce Foundation.

Another factor perhaps was the space age. It encouraged us to look to the heavens with a new spirit of adventure, to open our minds to new possibilities and certainly to broader horizons. It challenged science in ways that brought new concepts about the nature of the universe and the role of electrical or magnetic energies. At a 1987 conference in Madras, India the Nobel Prize–winning physicist Werner Heisenberg was reported to have concluded that "magnetic energy is that elementary energy upon which depends the whole life of the organism." But, said this distinguished scientist,

> No concerted appreciation of this fundamental force of nature seems to have been made, the attempts being sporadic and centered around individual thinkers who were not taken seriously. With the advent of the Space Age, the picture has changed totally. Scientists are now concerned more than ever before about the varieties of ways in which electromagnetic fields—both natural and man-made—interact with life at various levels, both beneficially and harmfully. . . . What is more, the beneficial aspects of Magnetism-Life interaction—as for example, the application of magnetic fields to medical therapy and diagnosis—are already under exploration.

Heisenberg was correct; the early theoreticians in energy medicine were virtually ignored, probably because most physicians simply could not understand *why* something as strange as electricity had any place in a body that was obviously biochemical in its makeup. Pictures of some of the early devices that made use of static electricity were also not very inviting, especially when they showed a frightened-looking patient whose hair was standing on end. The use of such electrical contraptions was also discouraged by the negative attitude of the federal Food and Drug Administration toward devices for which there is no scientific proof of the health benefits claimed. Although the FDA's supervision has fortunately cleared the marketplace of many quack products of yesteryear along with patent medicines that would "cure" practically every ailment, it has also made it difficult for people to try alternatives to drugs. Edgar Cayce suggested several devices, for example, which some people have used, apparently with good results. But lacking the standard proof of their therapeutic effects, anyone who manufactures or sells such appliances for medical purposes risks an encounter with the federal government. A friend of mine made these devices in his garage workshop for anyone who asked—he didn't advertise—and representatives of the FDA heard about it and came to his house one day asking to inspect the premises. My friend had gone on to his reward by then, and his widow refused to allow them to desecrate his good work by a posthumous search of his workshop unless they got a search warrant. They never returned.

Because of my faith in the wisdom of Edgar Cayce and in the effectiveness of the many therapies he recommended that we have used successfully with our patients, I have no doubt that the wet-cell appliance and the impedance device that he sometimes suggested have therapeutic benefits. Perhaps when we learn more about how and why energy medicine works we will yet be able to use them freely.

One pioneer researcher, Robert O. Becker, M.D., who was not discouraged by the lack of appreciation of the significance of electrical circuits in the body, has demonstrated the remarkable value of electromagnetic currents in the process of regeneration. He discovered this connection while exploring the remarkable power of the salamander to regenerate nearly all parts of its body. Scientists have puzzled over this phenomenon for centuries. Dr. Becker found that regeneration of a salamander's amputated leg comes about by means of a very weak electrical current that alters the cells in that area, rendering them more undifferentiated. Then the current redifferentiates the cells to produce the kind of tissue needed for rebuilding of the extremity—almost as if by magic.

Becker describes what happens first, after amputation. The cells in that area die. Then, there is a regrowth of the epidermis. This is very important, he says. The dermis, the deeper layer of the skin, does not grow over the cut surface, and the nerves in the vicinity grow into the epidermis and form a connection between each of the epidermal cells and threadlike bits of nerve tissue that is then called a neuroepidermal junction.

Then, cells that have dedifferentiated into a blastema form appear and begin to grow and divide into all the different tissues required to make up a new extremity that cannot be distinguished from the norm.

If, however, the nerve fibrils or the epidermis, either one, are interfered with so that the neuroepidermal junction is not formed, then regeneration will not take place. This interference can be done by surgically applying a skin graft or by interrupting the nerve supply. Allowing the epidermis to regrow itself and then being patient enough to allow the next step to take place without interfering makes for success.

In a lecture at a Healing Conference in Washington, D.C., in November 1981, Becker gave an account of work done in Vienna on salamanders, back in the middle and late 1960s. In Vienna,

> experiments focussed on *producing* a cancer in the salamander that would derive from its *own* cells, by repeated applications of a known carcinogenic substance, applied at the base of the tail.

> A skin cancer develops in the salamander which, if left untreated will also metastasize, and the animal will die. If, after metastasis, the tail is amputated, not *through* the tumor, but merely close by, the primary tumor disappears and, subsequently, all of the metastatic tumors disappear, and you're left with a completely salvaged salamander.

> We think, here, that what happens is that the tumor cells are completely de-differentiated back to primitive embryonal type cells, and re-used by the animal.

In view of the salamander's amazing ability to regenerate that tail and its tremendous need for embryonal cells in that area, one can begin to understand how that part of the body would use the cancer cells, dedifferentiate them into a more basic form and then reuse them to build a new tail. But what about the cancer islands in the various areas where the cancer has metastasized? Is this energy of regeneration an electrical current that flows through the entire body of the salamander, or do the cells in the various parts of the body go through the same process of dedifferentiation as those in the primary site of the cancer because of some distant communication process and close relationship that we currently do not even know exists?

There are obviously many questions about life, regeneration, healing, and the energy that flows through the living body that we have yet only touched upon. Much remains to be learned. What if, for instance, the energy of regeneration were to be introduced into the primary site of a tumor in a human being? Would those cells dedifferentiate? And would distant sites of metastatic cancer respond because the primary site changes? Or would the energy of regeneration need to be throughout the body to bring about change in cancer cells that have spread? Or do the salamander and the human have no relationship in this regard?

In our experience at the A.R.E. Clinic, in both our clinical applications and our research efforts, we still find the description of energy medicine in a formative stage. However, some clarity can be gained if we simply understand human beings as body, mind, and spirit. For the energy is life energy itself, the manifestation of the God-force, and is understood in the material world as electrical, electronic, electromagnetic, or magnetic energies. And in all its manifestation, whether generated inside or outside the body, it brings life to the human organism and healing when things are out of accord.

The potential for energy medicine, I feel sure, is great, and public awareness of it is increasing because of articles such as Kathleen McAuliffe's "I Sing the Body Electric," which appeared in December 1981 in *Omni* magazine. It said:

> We all wear an invisible garment, an electromagnetic cloak that shields us from head to toe. From the moment of conception, electrical currents begin to flow in the tiny embryo, guiding the incredibly delicate process that culminates in birth. When a salamander regrows a limb, similar currents flow along the injured extremity as if reenacting a crucial step of embryo-genesis. Once the new organism—or limb—is fully formed, the currents abate. Yet we all retain an electromagnetic halo as a birthday suit we carry throughout life.

The director of research programs at the A.R.E. Clinic, Harvey Grady, has noted how similar this concept, now accepted by scientists, is to that espoused over a half century ago by Edgar Cayce, who said: "The human body is made up of electronic vibration, with each atom and element of the body, each organ and organism of same, having its electronic . . . vibration necessary for the sustenance of and equilibrium in that particular organism" (1800–4).

Scientists now recognize that a healthy body depends upon an efficiently working electrical energy system. As the article in *Omni* put it, "Disturbances in these fields portend illness." Cayce said an injury or disease may result in deficient electronic energy, which is required for the equilibrium and sustenance of any element of the body.

A good example of the power of electrical impulses in energizing physical functions was the case of a man in Falmouth, Maine, who had gradually become both blind and deaf following an auto accident in 1971. In 1980 he had another accident—he was struck by lightning—but this time his senses benefited. Within an hour of receiving this electrical jolt, his vision returned; within a day his hearing was restored.

What seemed like a miracle was explained away by two skeptical doctors on the Harvard Medical School faculty who were asked to comment on how this could have happened. "Hysterical blindness," said one. "Hysterical deafness," said the other. In other words, the man had never lost his ability to see or hear; he just thought he had. "The hysterically blind get better when it is no longer in their best interest to be blind," explained the ophthalmologist. Neither of these doctors reportedly had conducted an examination, so they were speculating.

Their observations remind me of the neurologist who was asked about acupuncture during a television interview in 1972. It couldn't possibly work, he opined, because there was no neurological pathway in the skin through which such therapy could operate. He, of course, had not studied acupuncture.

My own work with acupuncture persuades me that it does work. We may not understand everything about how it works, or why it works; the theory is, however, that electricity does in fact pass through pathways in the skin where individual cells are more conductive that those on either side. These pathways are termed meridians, and scientific studies have now been conducted to substantiate such a theory. Whatever the explanation, patients of ours who have suffered a variety of pain conditions, medical problems such as appendicitis and heart conditions and a variety of other physical problems (which are described in the acupuncture literature extensively), have received relief from this therapy that "couldn't possibly work." I was pleased to see such a conservative publication as *Business Week* (May 4, 1987) report last year that "more and more doctors—

backed by a growing body of scientific evidence—are deciding that so-called 'alternative' or 'holistic' medicine is more than hocus-pocus. Among the once-controversial therapies gaining credibility: acupuncture, hypnosis, biofeedback, homeopathy, and creative visualization."

Research is the key to expanding the credibility of these and other new therapies. Even the federal government recognizes that. The National Institute of Health is sponsoring more than $70 million of research in behavioral medicine, which includes biofeedback, hypnosis, and relaxation training. With the assistance of a grant from the John E. Fetzer Foundation to expand our research, the A.R.E. Clinic established that Fetzer Energy Medicine Research Institute in 1984 and has launched a number of long-term investigations designed to document the energy patterns of the human body and gain a greater understanding of how they affect our health. The Cayce readings offer clues that must be taken seriously because of the correspondence we have already found between Cayce's biological concepts and what science has recently found to be true. Cayce, for example, said that all healing of every nature is the changing of the body's vibrations from within—the attuning of the Divine within the living tissues of a body to Creative Energies.

Like the early explorers looking for a shorter route from Europe to the Orient, we are looking for a more certain route to the land of perfect health. We are traveling uncharted waters when we consider Cayce's direction for "changing of the vibrations from within." We are moving beyond the body into the mind and spirit of the person. "Whether it is accomplished by the use of drugs, the knife, or what not," said Cayce, "it is the attuning of the atomic structure of the living cellular force to its spiritual heritage" (no. 1967–1).

"Electricity or vibration is that same energy, same power, ye call God," he added.

The titles of some of the papers presented at the International Energy Medicine Conference in India give you some sense of the direction current research is taking. Here are a few: The Electromagnetic Environment of Man; Pulsed Electromagnetic Fields in the Management of Head Injuries; Electromagnetic Hand Massage

Therapy; Parallels Between Yoga and Acupuncture Theory; The Relationship Between Electromagnetic and Psychic Energies; Kundalini Yoga and the Neurosciences; Laboratory Studies on Healing by Touch; and Energy Medicine in Indigenous Healing Systems.

From these we can glimpse the focus of the conference, from specific applications to the broad view. Both are needed. What is clear is the growing conviction that energy medicine is the wave of the future, that body energies hold the potential for healing miracles. R. M. Varna, emeritus professor of the National Institute of Mental Health and Neurosciences in Bangalore, India, sees energy as central to human health care:

> We find that in these three areas, i.e., the physical, the biological and the psychological, the model emerging is of a unitive and holistic one, with the substrate as energy and all phenomena as forms of transformation. The present day effort in the sciences in each one of the areas is to unravel the principles and the processes of transformation which are verifiable, workable and of utility.

To comprehend the energy factor we must learn more about vibrations, for creative vibration is the same energy as Life itself, according to Cayce.

Although a comprehensive description of energy medicine still lies in the future, perhaps it is a mechanism in the investigative and healing arts that will move us toward a greater understanding of what the practice of medicine should be about.

As that conference in Madras shows, throughout the world there is an awakening to the knowledge that human beings are indeed energy creatures. We all have a conscious and an unconscious mind, both of which work through the body systems with electromagnetic energies, and these facts must be taken into account in the advancement of the healing arts.

4

The Temple Beautiful

$\mathbf{M}$Y WIFE, GLADYS, AND I had been practicing medicine for twenty-two years and been researching Cayce for more than ten years when we opened the A.R.E. Clinic in 1970. We changed our approach from that of a conventional family practice into one that treats patients using Cayce's concepts of healing whenever they are applicable. We also conducted research at the clinical level with these concepts. We didn't limit ourselves to Cayce's explicit suggestions, but we supplemented the best medical knowledge available with his recommended therapies. We have treated the body, mind, and spirit of each patient as we understand what that means.

To focus our work, we adopted an ideal for the Clinic. Edgar Cayce had recommended that each person needs to adopt a set of ideals. You need to hold them in mind as you work out the details of your life, making sure *what* you do or *how* you live your life is harmonious with those ideals. We thought the Clinic would benefit by the same approach. Its ideals read like this:

> To manifest the Universal Christ Consciousness and to make manifest the love of God and man. Our ideal is to bring true healing to body,

mind, and spirit in helping individuals develop an awareness of their physical, mental, and spiritual potentials, thus establishing a more meaningful relationship with the Creative Forces of the Universe and a greater harmony with their fellow man.

As our understanding of the information in the Cayce readings expanded, we developed a variety of holistic therapies that seemed appropriate for the ailments our patients faced. We trained our staff, which grew from seven in 1970 to forty (plus volunteer workers) today, so that they were skilled in the application of these innovative therapies. The positive response of patients who had tried conventional medicine without success proved both exciting and rewarding. We knew then that Edgar Cayce's wisdom and his remedies were applicable to today's diseases and could help us combat tomorrow's as well.

For the first years we operated the Clinic in a fairly conventional manner, accepting patients as they came to us, offering only outpatient care, treating them as we saw them, and hoping they would stick with what we had recommended long enough for it to prove effective. We suspected that many patients found this difficult, especially when we asked them to change their diet radically. The impact on our health of the foods we routinely eat is powerful—and so are the habits we have developed and often pursue without thinking, whether it is drinking too much coffee, soft drinks, or worse, of eating fast foods on the run. We'll deal with diet and nutrition in more detail in the next chapter.

One of the inducements of today's conventional medicine for many patients is that it requires so little thought—three a day, one after each meal, is all the doctor often asks one to remember. And it often demands no real change in our life-style, including our bad eating habits. It is so easy that patients often go from one doctor to another, trying one drug after another, hoping to get lucky and be healed. When it works they are lucky indeed. But we think there is a better way, a surer way to find healing.

In 1978 we developed our own way of making it easy for our patients. We developed a residential program lasting seventeen days.

We call it the Temple Beautiful Program because in ancient Egypt, according to Cayce, there was a Temple Beautiful in which all kinds of therapies were applied beneficially.

The atmosphere of our "temple" is very homelike because we conduct it in a large residence located in a quiet neighborhood about a mile from the Clinic. It is thus removed from the clinical atmosphere, yet close enough for patients to keep appointments with our medical staff. And though much of the daily activity is centered in the Oak House, as we call it, almost everyone visits the Clinic daily for one or more therapeutic sessions, starting with a complete physical examination.

We limit the number of guests in each program to fifteen, the number we can comfortably house. When that many people gather around the dining room table for family-style meals or the living room for discussions, we seem to have a good mix and enough time for each person to receive his or her requisite attention. We soon feel like one big family as we eat together and open up to one another, confiding often in our new friends those deepest feelings that have a way of surfacing. What nearly everyone soon discovers is that this Temple Beautiful "family" is very accepting. Living in a caring community, even for a short while, is a novel experience for many people. This element of caring or loving concern provides a secret ingredient that is available to all who participate. That element of love can be very healing in its own way. Indeed, we think that love is a necessary ingredient to achieve full healing of the body, the mind, and the soul.

The word *love* is used to express various attractions—we love the mountains, we love to dance, we love home cooking and sports cars and on and on. These forms of "love" we find gratifying, self-gratifying. The love that heals, however, is something else. It is the love defined in the Bible. That form of love has no value unless applied to another person. It has to do with giving rather than getting. In that other person we see a reflection of ourselves and the presence of God. As we give love to another person, we love the God within that person, and in the process, we become more clearly attuned to the Infinite. The ultimate healing, or wholeness, is to be one with

God. The pathway to the goal is love. Not only do we need to follow that path but to teach others to follow it too.

This is not just theoretical. Love can be readily applied, no matter what the ailment or condition of the recipient. In one of our programs last year, for example, we had patients who were suffering from asthma, hypertension, premenstrual syndrome, Hodgkin's lymphoma, varicose veins, cancer of the uterus and cervix, Friedrich's ataxia, severe allergies, candidiasis, herpes simplex, and diabetes with visual impairment and detached retina. Such a variety of serious conditions in one group is not unusual. Though each one requires special care, they all respond to the basic therapy of loving concern. We begin the application when they arrive at Oak House. Smiles, warm greetings, and hugs make them feel at home quickly. They may not know it, but their therapy program has begun.

We are not talking here about just making people feel good. We are dealing with a basic law of life when we consider the effect of love. It attunes us to the Source of all life, and attunement brings health to the person suffering from dis-ease or even disease.

Each individual has the freedom to choose those elements that combine to form the patterns that reside in the spiritual-endocrine centers of the body. We choose the kind of emotions, attitudes, and beliefs that we wish to have. If they are not in attunement with our true spiritual nature, the consequence is lack of health through some sort of illness. Fortunately, healing is also available, if we so choose.

In pursuing the healing arts, we apply a variety of therapies, some suggested in the Cayce readings and some developed since he stopped giving information in 1945. They include massage, biofeedback, colonics, electromagnetic therapy, color and music therapy, and correcting of unconscious habit patterns of emotions, attitudes, and beliefs. Patients participate together in morning exercises, meditate as a group, and then over breakfast discuss one another's dreams recorded from the night before. Each person takes a turn at dinner telling his or her life story, which has a way of becoming much more than a light get-acquainted session. As often as not, people volunteer some deep feelings that they have carried alone for many years. Releasing feelings of childhood rejection or unrequited love or lack of self-esteem in a loving family atmosphere can be amazingly therapeutic.

Stress reduction is another objective of the Temple Beautiful Program. When we put together a variety of stress-reducing treatments—meditation, dream interpretation, a diet to balance the body, medication and vitamins as needed, and the kind of therapy that allows one to look at past-life experiences in a receptive and loving atmosphere—the results are often impressive. And that is true no matter what the other symptoms may be or which of the many forms of illness the individual has chosen. It illustrates the truth of Cayce's statement that "all healing comes from the One Source." He identified that source as the "Creative or God forces."

Power Within

In trying to understand the miracle of the healings that we have witnessed among our patients—people healed of cancer, asthma, gangrene of an extremity, scleroderma, arthritis, allergies, and even the common cold—I turned to the Bible as well as the Cayce readings. It has been a fascinating journey of discovery for me to find certain passages that offer new insights. One of them comes from the fourteenth chapter of John in the New Testament.

In the ninth and tenth verses, Jesus tells Philip that he, Philip, *had* seen the Father when he saw Jesus (Philip had wanted Jesus to show him the Father).

This statement of Jesus', equating himself with God, has confounded many people throughout the ages. But the last part of the tenth verse gave me an insight, and it helped me to explain healing of the physical body to myself and to others. Jesus then said, "the words that I speak unto you I speak not of myself: but the Father that dwelleth in me, he doeth the works." He went on to say that he was in the Father and the Father was in him. And later on he told his disciples that he would that they be one with him as he was one with the Father.

What it says to me is that our bodies certainly are the temples of God, and that God does indeed dwell therein—*in each one of us!* That just happens to be how we are put together.

If Jesus did not do the works, but "the Father, who dwelleth in me, He doeth the works," then something very important is being said to me. The work Jesus was talking about was the manifesting of love. For we are told that God is love. And we are told that we are to love God and love our fellow human beings—that's the whole law.

It seems to me that each time, then, that we love another person, we are not of ourselves loving that person but letting God love through us. If Jesus was in the position of having God love the world through him, then we are certainly no better than Jesus, and we must be letting God manifest through us when we are kind, when we are gentle, when we forgive, when we understand another, even when we tell a joke and laugh and bring joy. For all of these are the workings of love in our lives.

And so, I tell patients and the Temple Beautiful participants that if God is working through us when we do these things in relation to another person, then we certainly must be getting healthier, in the process of loving, because the very nature of God is bound to rub off on us, no matter how badly off we may be. That is a very important step in our healing. For love is an active force; it heals both those who give and those who receive love.

That is what begins when Erika greets the new patient warmly at the door of the Oak House with a smile and, more often than not, a hug. It is the working of Love (God) through her that begins the healing of the body-mind-spirit at that point.

Incidentally, hugging is a conscious part of the program. We follow the maxim that someone established—and we think is reasonable—that it takes four hugs a day for survival, eight for maintenance, and twelve for growth. In the programs, every morning after our meditation we take "time for hugs!"

We know that a hug is more than just a hug. It is sharing laughter, a joy that brightens up the day. But even more than that, it allows each participant to experience the touching, the laying on of hands, the sharing of the aura of another human being.

One can bring about healing in the body by consciously manifesting love instead of indifference. In keeping that choice active in belief patterns, the emotions one chooses to create, and the attitudes one forms as habit patterns, the unconscious mind gains light and clears out the darkness, while the seven spiritual centers become better balanced as they directly influence the seven major endocrine glands. Those same choices have a strong direct effect also on the coordination and balance of the organs and systems of the body, which bring life to the whole organism.

The touch has been shown by Dolores Krieger, R.N., to be a healing force—so much so that she has taught nurses in training about its importance and how to do it. (See her book, *The Therapeutic Touch: How to Use Your Hands to Help or Heal.*) We know that when one wants to be of service, even though it may be simply by touching another person, there is energy that comes out of the hands and acts to heal that other person. When both are desirous of helping, both experience the benefits of the healing touch. Remember, it is God working through us (when we make that commitment) to do that healing.

The laying on of hands has been known throughout the ages to be part of a proper healing effort. It starts in infancy when mothers hold their babies and rock them while they're crying. It is implemented a few years later when they fall down, scrape their knees, and come running to mother crying. Mother holds the child, puts her hand on the hurt knee for a few moments, then kisses the hurt spot. The healing is complete because of the love manifested through the touch.

Thousands of people, perhaps even millions, have helped their fellow human beings by practicing the art of the laying on of hands. This, of course, is usually accompanied by silent prayer and is understood to be more effective when it lasts for more than just a few moments. It is really an energy treatment, but best performed when one recognizes the Source of the energy that flows through the body and hands to the other person.

Once the Temple Beautiful program has begun and the greeting, the meditations, and the hugs have begun to work, we then understand that the participants begin to "reach out" with their auras (that energy/electromagnetic envelope that surrounds every living body), and contact and communication begins at a deeper level. The aura is that part of our original energy field "body" (which we have had from the very beginning) that extends in all directions beyond our physical framework. Some individuals can readily see the aura; most cannot. Those who see the aura state that anyone can learn how to see it. It's somewhat like what Edgar Cayce said about his abilities in the unconscious world, that anyone can do this. I'm sure that both claims are true, for we have innate within our own beings the creative powers of the universe. Remember, we were created in the image of God!

But Cayce had more to say. He indicated that powers would be granted to us if we had a good, constructive purpose in mind and would use the power in that direction. So, why do we want to see an aura? Why would we want to have the same abilities that Cayce had? What would we do with these if they became a part of our total being at the present time?

Why Be Healed?

In line with that same direction of questioning, we frequently ask our patients the same question that Cayce posed for some of those who sought out a reading. "Why do you want to get well? What will you do with your life if healing were completed right now?" In other words, what about the choices you have made in the past that built into your consciousness the attitudes and emotional patterns that have created the illness of your body? Are you doing something about recognizing what they are and changing them?

It is always important to become aware of those factors that create the disturbances in our bodies. It takes effort, often, and is highly disturbing at times, for what we have created in our bodies and our minds seems to us at the moment to be "normal." In other words, why isn't everyone else like me, since I'm "normal"? It requires honest looking, plus measuring those attitudes up against a standard that we choose to be our ideal or that toward which we wish to strive.

And when we find ourselves lacking, it hurts. And it hurts even more as we try to bring those errant activities into line with what we figure is right for us.

In a very real sense, we cannot *tell* another what his or her measuring stick should be, for each of us has to search that out for him- or herself. Jesus gave us a pattern to live by, but all may not interpret the detail of that pattern the same way, or even accept the Christ life as the ideal. Each entity in the earth *must* choose the path he or she is to take. And each one *does* do that, whether aware of it or not.

In our Temple Beautiful Program, however, many of the participants are already aware of the Cayce readings through having become members of the Association for Research and Enlightenment in Virginia Beach or through being patients at the Clinic locally. Most of the program patients come from distant states and countries because of the story of life and human adventure here on the earth as it was told in the readings.

These people, then, are ready for an investigation within themselves and are prepared for an adventure in consciousness. So the measuring up to the Christ as an ideal and accepting Jesus as the pattern of how to fulfill that concept of the Christ is already a familiar direction in which to look for help. They take to the hugs, the sharing of energies, the touch, the mixing of auras without difficulty.

Others, however, find it a challenge. Imagine how an engineer, steeped in the world of numbers, of theories, of research, and of things exactly arranged, would feel when a group of people he had never met before in his life started hugging him at the drop of a hat—he, who had difficulty hugging even his wife! Well, such individuals find that the true human nature emerges out of the depths—to their surprise—and life takes on a different hue. It is fascinating to watch such life-changing events take place in those who have been missing what life is all about for nearly all the years they have been around the earthly plane this time.

When the program gets started, we meet as a group for orientation and to get to know each other—or *begin* to know each other. At that time, we ask each one, "What do you hope to achieve out of this program?" Each person has a unique understanding of the question, and the answers are always different. Most of those who have a severe or life-threatening illness tell the group, with varying degrees of determination, "I'm going to overcome this illness!" And some of them do.

One cannot look inside the mind and the being of another person and tell when that person's adventure on the earth this time is going to come to an end. We talk about death freely, for it is in everyone's future, and the date is not rigidly set. But it *is* there. And when one looks at the true nature of each of us, one can understand why the spiritual realm is truly more our natural habitat than this time-structured material life on the earth.

Thus, with that basis set for communication and understanding among all of us, we can talk of past lives and how they might have influenced our present situation and responses thus far. We can talk about dipping into and out of the third dimension without hesitancy, recognizing that all of us think about life as a continuity, like a string of pearls, each pearl representing one life. And perhaps all the pearls are not of the same quality, but each tends to make a more beautiful string for the owner. We own the experiences of each lifetime, gathering the good and the creative qualities, leaving the destructive parts to be met later on or overcome with the aid in our lives of the secret ingredient we talked about earlier.

Gradually, the group of strangers becomes more like a gathering of old friends—and this sometimes begins to happen in just a few hours. It is almost as if they were drawn together for a reason, perhaps to renew old aquaintances from past lives or a certain past life when all their lives may have crossed.

It is not at this point, however, that we ask the hard question about the "why" of being healed. That comes later on, when many of the defenses have been dropped, and individuals—in their own specific time—are ready to deal with such a problem. Some do it much earlier than others.

People find, soon after arrival, that they may have a roommate, or perhaps two or three. Some are used to living alone, and it becomes a challenge for them to adjust. Nearly every time this happens, those who want to object the most find that their unwanted roommate turns out to be a dearly beloved friend from the distant past, or a sister or brother or co-worker on a project ended hundreds of years ago.

One group, composed almost entirely of women, turned up the information from their dreams and experiences that they had all been together in a convent several hundred years ago in Spain. And they had all taken a vow of silence at that time. Needless to say, mealtimes were very quiet in this gathering of souls. But they were not uncomfortable in the silence—rather, they moved into it very naturally. One of the group was a nun in this lifetime.

It was not difficult for members of this group to understand early on that they were searching for healing so that they might—in their own way—be of better service to someone.

But by the time the orientation day is finished, most of those who come to these programs recognize that they are in a loving, accepting, and supportive environment that allows them to share fears and hates, disturbance and losses, that they have kept hidden for years and years, afraid that if they expressed them they would be looked at as strange or be criticized or ostracized. It allows hidden problems to surface and makes for the continuation of the total healing process that began with a smile and a hug.

In all our programs, we tell our life stories. Some are long, some short, but everyone gets a chance to share his or her life experiences. One woman who came to the program because she had developed cancer of the uterus told her story the very first evening. To a group of people who had been simply strangers just a few hours earlier, she revealed that her father, who was then deceased, had sexually "used" her over a period of years while her mother fearfully turned away from what she thought was happening.

The caring and concern expressed by her newfound friends—this was the first time she had ever told anyone—was a major factor in helping her to acquire a better understanding of herself and in starting her on a course of healing. Added to her previous course of chemotherapy, it appeared to point her toward a life free of the fear she had experienced with the cancer and allowed her to overcome her illness totally.

What Was the Real Temple Beautiful?

When a group of us from the clinic visited Egypt in 1978, our guide stood in front of the Sphinx, near the Great Pyramid, pointed to a spot not far away, and said, "And that's where the Temple Beautiful stood!"

Much information is found in the Edgar Cayce readings about both the Temple Beautiful and the Temple of Sacrifice. According to this source of information, during the time shortly before the final sinking of Atlantis—about 10,500 B.C.—the priest Ra-Ta set up these temples for purposes of purification. From these readings emerges a picture of spiritual human beings merging with animals in the earthly plane—becoming part of them, in a sense—and eventually becoming trapped in their bodies. Gradually there developed beings that were half-man, half-animal, the centaurs, the sphinx, the mermaid, and creatures who were more one than the other, who wore feathers or wings, who had horns or hooves.

Even today medical science occasionally encounters such a being. In 1982 the *New England Journal of Medicine* reported on a case of a newborn child who came into this world with a two-inch-long tail. The *Journal* reported that it was a "well-formed caudal appendage . . . covered by skin of normal texture and had a soft, fibrous consistency." Located at the end of the spine, it had hair and nerves but no bone or cartilage. It was surgically removed.

The doctor reporting the case, Fred D. Ledley, M.D., said that the occurrence of a tail like this has been reported in hundreds of instances since 1850 and that such reports achieved special prominence during the debates over Darwin's theory of evolution. In addition to being incongruous, Ledley pointed out that it raises issues that involve not only embryology, but also our view of ourselves and our place in evolution.

We sometimes see other evidence of Darwin's evolution—individuals are born with skin that is so much like fish scales that it is called icthyosis, and there are people who have lumps like horns on their heads.

The Cayce readings also lead us to believe that the animal nature that was exteriorized in those days has gradually become internalized over the ages into ailments of the body and difficulties of the mind. Horns, for instance, he said, have been transformed into habits—our bullheaded way of doing things.

Purification in those days came about through surgery in the Temple of Sacrifice and through work in the Temple Beautiful on the mind, on the emotions, and on spiritual upliftment. Today it comes about in the process of establishing new habits that are constructive and letting go of those that are destructive.

The intent of purification then, it appears, was to correct the external nature of human beings that had become so entangled with the animals. Today it is to work with those same animal natures that have been internalized into the patterns of our emotions, our attitudes, and our beliefs—all of which we have chosen. Do you know someone who is stubborn as a mule? Or bullheaded? Or strong as a horse? Or chicken-hearted? You can name others.

But what about these two temples back in those ancient times, when Atlantis was sinking into the ocean? Just what were they like, and what happened inside those temples? One description of the structure of the Temple Beautiful indicated that it was in the shape of an inverted egg placed within a pyramid, much like as shown below.

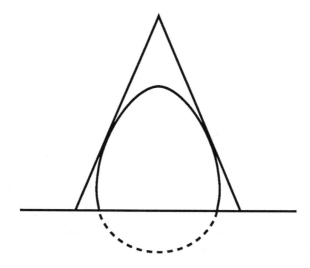

The best way to gain better insights on these two temples, however, is to quote several of the passages from Cayce's readings that describe life in those times:

> As has been indicated, in that particular experience there were still those who were physically entangled in the animal kingdom with appendages, with cloven hoofs, with four legs, with portions of trees, with tail, with scales, with those various things that thought forms (or evil) had so indulged in as to separate the purpose of God's creation of man, as man—not as animal but as man. And the animal seeks only gratifying of self, the preservation of life, the satisfying of appetites. With infinity injected in same brought the many confused activities or thoughts that we know now as appetites. Yes, a dog may learn to smoke! Yes, a horse may learn to eat sugar! But these are not natural inclinations—rather man's influence upon these activities by associations!
>
> All these forms, then, took those activities in the physical beings of individuals. This priest, this Ra-Ta, attempted to eradicate same; in that manner as might be compared to the hospitalization in the present, where individuals—through the lack of the proper application of the physical laws—have allowed growths, tumors, cancers, those things or conditions in the body,—stones in various portions of the organism; and then necessity—as considered in the present—of operative measures to remove growths of various characters throughout the system. Then these had more the form of activities that were outward manifestations. Now they have gradually been subsided, to be sure; yet these nearer illustrate the character of the things attempted to be eradicated. Not that it was wholly, wholly the truth, but the best understanding to that period. (no. 2072–8)

In another reading, for a fifty-three-year-old woman who was writing a book about these abnormalities, Cayce added that surgery was not the only means of coping with animal appendages.

> There was also the preparation of individuals through reading and through the application of the laws of diet, as to make such appendages be gradually released entirely from certain types of individuals. Only those who had mixed with the thought forms had same, you see. (no. 2067–6)

Still another reading reported that a seventeen-year-old Libyan princess named Ai-Si became acquainted with Ra-Ta while he was in exile in her country. While there, the priest apparently was practicing some of the methods that were later used in both the Temple of Sacrifice and the Temple Beautiful. And the princess became very adept at teaching dance, music, and diet. She had gone through a purification process and a learning of many lessons so that she would become a teacher of others in the same studies. As her studies continued, then she became what we would call today a nutritionist, being expert in all aspects of the preparation of food. She was also among the first users of the harp as she taught others rhythm and dance in the temple worship.

Our modern-day Temple Beautiful does not duplicate the old one. There seems no present need to fulfill a task like that. But with music, diet, dance, and the meditation that was practiced in those former days, there is a resemblance. And we tell our participants that the real Temple Beautiful is their own body. There is where they meet the Divine within.

Today's Temple of Sacrifice is to be found wherever people place their bodies on the altar called an operating table and allow the priest to remove the gallbladder, or the appendix, or the uterus. And, in the process, if their desires and wishes are in the right direction, they will there be healed.

We encourage all program participants to be open to flashes of past lives that may come into their consciousness at times, for we know that each soul needs to look at the past for understanding and should, as Cayce suggested, look to the future with hope. But when we touch in to a past incarnation in which we gained much by helping others, our ability to know what was truly known in that experience is aroused, so that search can be valuable to us in the present.

Another individual who had an incarnation during those days in Egypt was given an answer that can be deeply meaningful to each of us, if we truly take it to heart. Cayce said:

All knowledge,—then, now, or in the future,—is latent within self,—would man but begin to understand. The stamp, the image of the

Creator is a part of the heritage of each soul. Thus all knowledge that has been is a part of the experience of the soul. The entity here. . . . sought that knowledge in self, by its experience of unfoldment. (no. 2533–4)

In a later reading given for the person who had been Ai-Si, the Libyan princess associated with Ra-Ta, she was told something more about what she did in the temples. For she worked in both. She had the ability to tune in with the music of her viola to the forces of nature that are destructive, and burn out those desires that separate human beings from the creative forces. Her use of the dance in the movement of the body in every motion that brought a tuning in—in a sense— helped to bring to those who wanted to rid themselves of the animal nature an upliftment, a movement of the creative forces along "that which is set within the inner man as that cord of life that once severed may separate, does separate, that balance between the mind, the body, the soul" (no. 2533–6).

In the Temple Beautiful, the dance and the incantations she used made the changes within so that there might come, as it were, "the sound as of many waters; or as the morning stars in their circuit about the earth may sing with the glorious coming of the light into the experience of man to raise same to his at-oneness and his attunement with those beauties of the coming of the sons of men into the earth that God in His Oneness of Purpose may bring those activities with the sons of God as an at-onement in *their* purposes in the earth."

In many ways, we still need to bring about within ourselves a greater balance between mind, body, and soul in order to be healed. Meditations, prayers, creative dance, and incantations can all help this process in any modern Temple Beautiful. But we can best find healing through our relationships, through serving our fellow human beings.

PART II

Healing Your Body

5

Healing
Through Nutrition

WITHIN THREE HOURS OF the time participants in the Temple
Beautiful Program arrive at the Oak House, they take part in their
first meal together. From that point on, one of the major topics of
conversation is food.

The basis of all the meals served at Oak House is that the food is
the best that can be found. It is as fresh as can be arranged; it is
cooked wisely; and it is served in a manner that delights the palate
and the eye.

Some years ago, we developed at the clinic a basic diet (see chart
in Appendix) formulated from nutritional advice found in the Cayce
readings. A diet is always a part of our therapy program for anyone
who comes to the Clinic for care. It may be a simple change from
fried foods to baked or broiled, or it may be adding a fresh green
salad to the usual regimen. Avoidance of food in order to lose weight
is paramount for some. Occasionally, one needs to gain weight. Others, who have developed cancer or hypoglycemia or candidiasis, are
each given special diets. Or we may find that the patient is already on
a diet that is constructive in his or her special situation.

Always, however, we point out that what one takes into one's

.nuing nutrition. And that, along with what we think,
..y makes us what we are. So diet is very important.

In the basic diet, suggestions can be simplified. Following the diet
needn't be a laborious project. And this could be applied to nearly
any condition of illness in the human body:

1. No fried foods (except occasional bacon fried *very* crisp).
2. No white flour or white sugar products.
3. Do not combine cereals and citrus products at breakfast.
4. Make your lunch a large fresh green salad. A light dressing is
   preferable. Add soup if desired.
5. Eat fish, fowl, or lamb for protein, no pork, only occasional
   beef.

No single diet, of course, is applicable worldwide, or even in one's
own country. It is probably wise to remember what Jesus indicated
to his disciples when he sent them out. He told them to eat what is
served—that no food is bad, since it is part of God's creation. What
comes out of the mouth is more important than what goes in. For the
food goes to the gut and eventually passes out, but what comes out
of the mouth comes from the heart. And that's where we keep our
angers, our prejudices, our regrets, our jealousies, and those other
things that crowd into our unconscious minds, ready to be called
upon when we want to rebel against one of the laws of the earth or
the heavens; or when we once more act out the animal part of our
nature, to survive, or to get even, or simply to have our way.

Thus, this basic diet and its variations (always remembering that
there will be those times when guidance from within directs us on
matters of eating) become the manner in which we work with foods
with our patients, both in the programs and in the outpatient
department.

When we have cancer patients at the Clinic, we usually start them
on a diet that is a variation or a relaxed version of the diet that Cayce
suggested for several individuals with cancer. He told them to take
the foods that a cow or a rabbit would eat. Sometimes patients will
follow such a nutritional program.

One lady who came to the clinic from Virginia had been diagnosed as having cancer of the rectum. Surgery was advised: an abdominal-perineal resection, which would remove the large bowel from midway in the descending colon through the rectum, leaving her with a permanent abdominal colostomy. As a registered nurse, she knew what this sort of thing meant, and refused the surgery.

She also knew about the Cayce work and moved to Phoenix for thirteen months in order to apply the therapies he suggested. The most difficult treatment was the diet, because what she ate was up to her. The other therapies, such as massage and colonics, working with her dreams, and so on were done for her by others.

She adopted a diet of raw green vegetables, without salad dressing, and herbal tea and water—nothing else for nearly nine months. Her weight dropped from about 150 to 123 and stayed there. That was her basic weight. When she put into her mind the thought that the cow or rabbit is content eating that kind of a diet, she could, if she wished, be content too. After nine months she gradually increased her raw food intake to include blueberries, then other fruit. She added cooked vegetables a bit later on.

During the process, she had many dreams of encouragement. They helped a lot.

The cancer gradually isolated itself, became pedunculated (almost like a small appendix), and was then removed simply by a surgeon who treated the area twice with silver nitrate. That was in 1968, and the gracious lady is still healthy.

The diet is where we always begin our program of therapy. Nothing except human relations takes up more of our time or our interest. We all sleep six to eight hours every night, but we are usually not conscious of what goes on during sleep—it only comes to us sometimes in dreams. But we feed our bodies with food three times (or more) daily, and much time and thought goes into the preparation and the taking in of this substance that becomes a storehouse of energy for keeping us healthy and rebuilding all the tissues of the body.

A twenty-three-year-old woman came into our Temple Beautiful Program several years ago having been diagnosed with lupus erythematosus and not responding to the treatment she was getting. A highly alkaline diet was prescribed for her as the program began, and she stayed on it strictly. One can rarely pin down just one therapy as causing a response in the body, but in her instance the diet was probably the dominant factor in the response she made. She was on no medication, but she was taking part, of course, in all the other therapies in the program, including daily meditation, the use of castor oil packs, group therapy, electromagnetic field treatments, massage, guided imagery, the music and color sessions, and dream study. But it must be emphasized again, the diet was primary in her instance.

What happened? At the beginning of the program, the results of her blood enzyme tests were so grossly abnormal that they were repeated in ten days. These are the results:

	July 17	July 27	Normal
Alkaline phosphatase	487 U/L	157 U/L	30–115
GGT	146 U/L	65 U/L	0–45
SGOT	760 U/L	39 U/L	0–41
SGPT	280 U/L	53 U/L	0–45
LDH	700 U/L	431 U/L	100–225

Those who are acquainted with laboratory findings appreciate the changes shown here. They revealed that the liver was functioning much more efficiently on July 27 than ten days earlier. A response such as this is not only unusual, it is quite startling—and gratifying to the patient, to the doctor.

The food she was given carried the elements needed to rebuild portions of her body so that they could function properly. After ten days they were close to a normal balance—it's the balance that is always needed. And her diet was simply the basic diet, adhered to strictly.

Another cancer patient came to us just two months after she had been operated on for cancer of the tongue with one lymph node found already with metastatic cancer cells. She was advised to have further therapy after surgery, but she opted rather to come to the Temple Beautiful Program first.

She was instructed to cut her coffee to one cup a day and to stop all alcohol intake; she had been averaging more than two beers daily.

She was placed on a modified cancer diet, which
some resistance. The lesion, and the affected lymp
had been removed, so her general condition was fa
home, convinced that she was on the way to complete rec
would have no recurrence.

Rechecks with her doctors at home showed no problem in the
months following surgery. When she was seen at the Clinic two years
after her initial visit, she was up a bit in weight, but feeling well and
doing well. She had developed some canker sores in her mouth because of dietary indiscretions. She was still taking some alcohol, although very little.

Her cholesterol had elevated a bit; she had started taking some
medication for her blood pressure, which she was trying to discon-
tinue; and her blood sugar and uric acid were slightly elevated—
nothing really remarkable, but changing her life-style and diet had
given her a bit of trouble. Her story demonstrates, however, that one
needs to continue the constructive therapy in the body until the mind-
emotion part of oneself is balanced and in a healing mode.

Diet is largely responsible for the cholesterol level. The triglycerides in the bloodstream are regularly reported with the serum cholesterol as indicators of the tendency (or lack of it) for hardening of the
arteries with resultant heart disease or stroke. Much research has
been conducted on the relationship between these illnesses and the
fatty substances in the bloodstream.

Several years ago three instances of a rather remarkable change
in the blood levels of triglycerides among my patients at the Clinic
came to my attention. One showed dietary changes over a period of
four months; the other two showed changes in only four days.

Most remarkable benefit was noted in a thirty-four-year-old
man, who, at 210 pounds, was overweight for his six-foot height. In
October of 1984, he had a triglyceride level of 754 (normal is 100–
200). He was advised to cut his alcohol down from three beers a day
to one or none if possible, decrease coffee from eight cups to two
cups daily, adopt a low-fat diet, and add niacin, vitamins C and E,
and zinc to his daily regimen. And he was advised to do aerobic
exercises.

In four months, his triglycerides had dropped from 754 to 235—still a bit high, but remarkably changed. His serum cholesterol had decreased from 223 to 190, but his weight was down just four pounds. He had changed his diet only moderately—enough to alter the ominous results of his blood tests, but not enough to drop many pounds.

The other two instances involved a man and a woman who were participants in one of our Temple Beautiful programs. Both of these people were given diets strictly in accordance with the suggestions in the Cayce readings. On Monday of their nine-day stay in the Oak House, fasting blood specimens were taken, and on Friday of the same week, they were repeated, also in a fasting state.

The woman, who had no fish or fowl or other protein in the four-day period, showed triglyceride reading changes from 497 to 184. The man, who did have fish and fowl during those four days, saw his triglycerides change from 237 to 188. I tell my patients that it's preferable to have a triglyceride reading of 100 or below, although most laboratories report a normal reading under 150 milligrams. So these two were not down to normal yet, but were much improved.

The National Cancer Institute in Washington has reported that 60 percent of the cancers in women and 40 percent of those in men are caused by dietary habits. The Institute advocates eliminating fats, processed foods, and heavy intake of meat and eating lots of green vegetables, fresh fruits, and fish and fowl for protein. It's the same basic diet the Cayce readings have been suggesting for nearly three-quarters of a century. The researchers also suggest increasing vitamin A and C and selenium in the diet. I think it is obvious that a diet that prevents cancer will at the same time make for a healthier body and less illness of any sort.

Information about what might bring healing to the body is, when not in printed form, fortunately, neither limited nor censored. It appears to be intuitively perceived, a thought-form, a reality that then becomes available to other minds—sometimes throughout the world—especially to those who are seeking that information. A woman who was not in any of our programs wrote to me about a Japanese friend whose eleven-year-old son had developed a large malignant tumor on his head. He had received chemotherapy that had made him quite ill and caused him to lose his hair.

The boy's mother then heard of the benefits of raw food.

Every other day she shopped for ten crates of fresh, raw vegetables (carrots, celery, kale, cabbage, etc.), and carefully washed and dried each piece. Every day she put five crates of vegetables through the juicer and gave the juice to her son to drink.

The boy did not like all the juice, but she gave him no choice. She also gave him cooked brown rice, soy curd, and occasionally freshly made apple juice for something sweet (no meat and no dairy foods). The rest of the family objected and complained, but somehow she carried on this routine.

After a month the boy showed some improvement, and after eighteen months the tumor was gone. The boy was re-examined by his doctors, and they could find no trace of cancer or tumor. So the boy returned to school and was even allowed to get on the track team.

I can vouch for the value of vegetables, freshly juiced. We give this routinely to all our cancer patients in our special programs. They get it without even asking.

Almonds are another staple we recommend. There are always almonds on the breakfast table at Oak House for anyone to take. Cayce suggested much value in eating them, so they are available daily. Another story that came to me from my correspondence is related to almonds and to tumors. This tumor apparently was nonmalignant, although it was not tested. "In 1975," Bill Donato relates,

I noticed a growth on my back. Concerned, I visited my family physician, who told me that the lump on my spine was a "fatty tumor," and hence benign. He said that the only reason for removing it would be for cosmetic purposes. I had more or less resigned myself to an operation in a few months. I had read what the Edgar Cayce readings had said about almonds and thought that I really didn't have anything to lose since the tumor seemed to be getting bigger. In profile, it reminded me of a goose egg.

I started eating almonds at breakfast until I was eating forty a day every day. After a while, it didn't seem to be getting any bigger. After

١ine months (approximately) I thought the tumor looked a
er. My mother confirmed it. It kept on shrinking. To all
...cuts and purposes, it was gone in just a few months more. I
sometimes find it difficult even to find the area where it was.

During this time the only change in my lifestyle was the addition of
almonds, and sometimes grape juice. Grape juice was also mentioned in
one of the readings. . . . The tumor seemed to shrink a little faster when
I was using both.

At Oak House, we also use herbal teas, including the South American pau d'arco, the southwestern desert chaparral tea, and a variety of others. And we have used wheatgrass and barley green for those who are trying to overcome cancer in their systems.

Since healing is achieved by awakening the cells within to their divine origin, we try to take advantage of all those substances that will work toward that end.

Every individual who comes to my attention who has had any indication of heart difficulty is advised to take some olive oil every day. Olive oil has been used beneficially wherever it is available, notably in the Mediterranean countries. Residents of these olive-producing areas who make that oil a staple in their diet have a heart disease rate far lower than in the rest of the European population.

A professor of medicine and biochemistry at the University of Texas in Dallas, Dr. Scott Grundy, has found that olive oil, a monounsaturated fat, has several advantages over the group known as polyunsaturates—corn oil, soybean oil, safflower, and others. The effect on the body of polyunsaturates is to remove the high-density lipoprotein (HDL), which is beneficial in protecting the body, as well as the low-density lipoprotein (LDL) that is dangerous to the body.

Olive oil, on the other hand, sends the LDL to the liver to be detoxified while selectively increasing the HDL. Another benefit is in its degree of saturation. Being monounsaturated, olive oil is less vulnerable to oxidation than the polyunsaturated oils, thus reducing its tendency to become rancid, even in the bloodstream. This leads to less formation of the unstable molecules, or free radicals, as they are called, that are believed to be an important cause of cancer.

Both the HDL and the LDL levels are used widely in helping to predict the possibility of heart disease. The less of the LDL and the more of the HDL one has in the bloodstream in relationship to cholesterol, the less chance one has of suffering a heart attack. In some laboratories, this is called a coronary risk profile.

Cayce suggested that olive oil most often should be taken in very small doses, half a teaspoonful at a time, perhaps every two or three hours, depending on what is being treated. He recommended the use of olive oil as part of the treatment of general debilitation where blood building was needed. He suggested its use also for problems with assimilation and elimination, for excess acidity in the stomach and intestinal tract, and for colitis, anemia, epilepsy, and tendencies toward cancer or tumors.

It is always interesting to observe how Cayce saw things happening in the interior of the body—in its physiological functioning. His direction was always toward rendering the body and its systems back to a more normal condition. The readings that follow help to understand what he was suggesting. For a woman who was generally debilitated and in need of blood building, Cayce said:

> We would give a diet that is easily assimilated. We would take all the olive oil we are able to assimilate, in very small doses. This may be taken two, three, four, five times each day—half a teaspoon. (no. 3842–1)

for a man who was having problems of assimilation and elimination and overacidity, Cayce recommended:

> Very small doses of olive oil would be well to be taken. This should be taken often. Very small doses, meaning three or four drops to five drops at a time, not more than that. That is just enough to produce those activities in the gastric flow along throughout the esophagus and through the upper portion of the stomach, so that the activities with same will make for the enlivening of a food to the walls of the digestive force and system itself. (no. 843–1)

Cayce recommended that "olive oil in *small* quantities is *always* good for the whole of the intestinal system" (no. 846–1). He also said that "pure olive, half a teaspoonful twice a day . . . will aid digestion and the activity of the liver in aiding in blood building (no. 5604–1).

Small doses are to help the intestinal tract function better. Larger quantities of olive oil were often recommended after a series of castor oil packs to the abdomen. As I understand that suggestion, it is to stimulate the liver and gall bladder to pour out their contents, to a large degree, after these organs have been "awakened," in a sense, by the castor oil packs.

It is probably reasonable also to assume that a more efficiently functioning assimilating system will render the bloodstream, the eliminations, and the circulation in general into a more health-producing state. We must remember that coordination within the body is always concerned with consciousness and the process of maintaining balance and cooperation.

One can generally develop a diet around the concepts already discussed. Two examples will be found in the Appendix. The Bibliography includes recommendations for additional reading on diet and nutrition concepts found in the Cayce readings. For nothing is more basic to good health and to healing than the foods we choose every day.

6

The Acid-Alkaline Balance

In all systems of the body, in all functions of the body, there must be a balance in order to achieve health or a state of reasonable equilibrium. It is also desirable to achieve a balance between the acid and alkaline components in the body.

The balance between these two important substances is expressed as the pH of the blood, the hydrogen ion concentration. The pH factor reveals whether a tissue or a fluid is on the alkaline or the acid side of things. An imbalance on the acid side can cause many difficulties. A ten-month-old child was brought into the Clinic recently who had been in the hospital numerous times since birth with repeated infections of the respiratory tract. She slept poorly at night, and the mother was desperate. Antibiotics did nothing but let the child develop a case of thrush—a yeast infection that coats the tongue with a whitish color.

Dr. Gladys, the attending physician in the Clinic, gave the mother strict advice regarding the diet: lots of alkaline-reacting foods, few sweets or starches, and no milk for the present. Almost immediately the child's sleep began to improve, and there were fewer and shorter episodes of upper respiratory trouble. Within just a few weeks, the child looked and acted normal—no more trips to the hospital, and fewer troubles with the throat and lungs.

The diet that Dr. Gladys recommended created a more alkaline condition in the child's body. As Cayce mentioned a number of times, if the diet is more alkaline, it's difficult to get a cold or an infection.

By the time the Temple Beautiful people are gathered for their first breakfast together, they have seen two meals served and have questions about choices of food. The question of acid and alkaline arises. Which are acid foods and which are alkaline? A short answer is provided in the following lists:

Alkaline	Acid
Vegetables	Starches
Fruits	Sugars
Fruit and vegetable juices	Most meats
	Fats

—Milk is neither or both,—
acid or alkaline

For every rule set up, there are always exceptions. Don't take the foregoing list as absolute, but as a general guideline. Citrus fruit, for instance, is high in citric acid, but is alkaline-reacting in the body. Milk can be different in its reaction depending upon the amount of butterfat it contains. A small booklet entitled *Foods That Preserve the Alkaline Reserve* provides a good guide to this information (see Appendix).

Combining different foods complicates things. Cayce suggests that combinations of certain foods, such as fats and sugars, can create more acidity in the system than either one alone. A good diet is not 50-50 acid-alkaline foods, Cayce said, but "about twenty percent acid to eighty percent alkaline-producing" (no. 1523–3). People who work or play hard physically can tolerate more acids than those in more sedentary life-styles. Cayce explained it like this:

> For, in all bodies, the less activities there are in physical exercise or manual activity, the greater should be the alkaline-reacting foods taken. *Energies* or activities may burn acids, but those who lead the sedentary

life or the non-active life can't go on sweets or to
these should be well balanced. (no. 798–1)

Time and time again, for various condition
vegetables that grow under the ground, as well as い
fruits, and nuts, should form a greater part of the regular diet.

One of the important benefits of maintaining alkalinity is prevention of illness. When he was asked about immunization against contagious diseases, Cayce said, "If an alkalinity is maintained in the system—especially with lettuce, carrots and celery, these in the blood supply will maintain such a condition as to immunize a person" (no. 480–19).

These admonitions to favor alkalinity in the diet should not be taken to extreme. As Cayce said:

> This does not necessitate that there should *never* be any of the acid-forming foods included in the diet; for an overalkalinity is much more harmful than a little tendency occasionally for acidity. But remember there are those tendencies in the system for cold and congestion to affect the body, and cold *cannot—does not—*exist in alkalines. (no. 808–3)

From these comments, one can see that keeping a proper balance either in the physical body or in the foods that are taken is not a simple matter. Consider what happens in a young person whose diet is mostly soft drinks, milk shakes, hamburgers, candy, cake, and ice cream, plus dry cereal and milk in the morning. There is always a reaction in the body to one's diet. So in the near or distant future, depending upon the activities of the body and the natural tendencies to stay healthy, the body will pay a price.

Why an Alkaline Diet?

Why should an alkaline diet be preferable to an acid-reacting one? What happens in the human body when foods of one nature or another are assimilated? What impact does this have upon the bloodstream, for instance? Or the immune system? Or the digestive tract? Is the diet the only factor influencing all these functional parts of the nan being? Or can thoughts or emotions, reactions to situations, lay a part in creating acidity? Does exercise help to bring a balance? What about sleep? Does a smile change the pH in the body tissues or fluids?

Although medical science cannot answer all these questions— and has not even asked all of them—we at the clinic have found satisfactory answers to most of them. They are satisfactory because they help us with our patient care. In answering questions for individuals who came to him for readings, Cayce approached these questions in the light of "How do we care for this person, so that he will be brought back to health?" That is the clinical way of doing things— but Cayce worked at it with the understanding that it is the cells and the organs of the body that must do the work of supporting and enhancing life in this organism we call the human body.

Thus, the environment of those cells, organs, and systems must be considered; the surroundings of these parts must be conducive to life and health, or they will be adversely affected. One cannot live in a filthy environment long and not be affected by it. The pH of the blood, the lymph, and the cells throughout the body, then, is a major part of the internal environment.

Perhaps the most immediate answer to the question "Why an alkaline diet?" would be that it aids the immune system, which is the protector of the entire body. Clinical evidence supports this theory. The diet recommended by the American Cancer Society as a factor in avoiding cancer is an alkaline-reacting diet.

When one is placed on a diet such as Cayce suggests, the immune system is bolstered, brought up to strength, so that one simply does not get the illnesses that one did on a meat and potatoes diet, with bread and gravy, and apple pie with ice cream for dessert.

The immune system includes the thymus gland as the master of the whole system and the lymphatic structures like the tonsils and adenoids, the appendix, the Peyer's patches, and the lymph nodes distributed throughout the body. Other parts of the immune system are the liver, the spleen, the bone marrow, and all the lymphatic vessels with their contents. The lymph stream not only helps to defend the body, but also carries hormones from all the hormone-producing cells. The lymphatics also provide the first step in elimination, carrying waste products from each cell to the large veins of the body, thence to the arterial stream, and finally to the four organs of elimination: the liver/intestinal tract, the kidneys, the lungs, and the skin. They all do their part in cleansing the body.

The lymphatics provide a unique structure in the body, distinct from the circulatory stream, where the arteries end up as arterial capillaries, which become venous capillaries, then larger and larger veins until the blood is carried to the heart and recirculated through the lungs and out through the arteries again to the entire body. The lymph system is not like that. A rough drawing would show the continuation of the arterial, then venous, capillaries flowing through the extracellular spaces, which are partially filled with interstitial tissue (there is usually enough space free to allow investigating lymphocytes to make their way!), near the cell or cells they supply with life substances like oxygen and food molecules. The lymphatics are like rivers that have their beginning far from their destination. Unlike the blood, the lymphatics run in one direction only. A river begins with a drop of rain falling on a mountain that gathers other drops and rivulets and such to make a stream, or it may start like the Mississippi, by gathering water from inside the earth and then taking on other small streams to finally make a river.

The lymphatic capillaries begin as little blind sacs, open on only one end, and they continue as vessels, taking fluid from the interstitial spaces in the body. The small vessels join and become larger until the entire flow is emptied into the body's counterpart of the Gulf of Mexico: the large veins directly above the heart.

The lymph provides protection for the body, it acts as a carrier for hormones and chemical messages from cells throughout the body to other cells, and in addition it performs an essential function of elimination.

For those who wish to study the lymphatics deeply, *Lymphatics and Lymph Circulation*, written by three researchers in Budapest, is exhaustive in its information, covering research that has extended over three centuries. It also includes an extensive bibliography. You can find the details in the Bibliography at the back of this book.

When we overindulge in acid-ash foods, the lymphatic system has to deal with it. The bloodstream has a pH of 7.34 and the lymph 7.41. These are fairly constant, but apparently the blood has priority on maintaining that level. The lymph is left with what the blood discards. Thus, if a highly acid diet is consumed, and much of that acid is absorbed into the bloodstream, the blood has to do something with it. So it's passed on to the lymph, thence to the cells or to the body's eliminatory channels.

If this is a chronic situation, and the cells of the body become overacid, then the lymph becomes overburdened and its pH goes down. At that point the immune capacity of the lymphocytes and other protective substances in the lymph is hampered by the change in the acidity of their environment, and thus the resistance of the entire body is lowered to all kinds of organisms that might then cause difficulty. At the same time, the cells with lowered pH (i.e., overacid) will not function normally. They might then "go wild," in a sense, and become malignant. We haven't fully answered the question of why a normal cell of the body becomes malignant and tries to destroy the rest of the body. Somewhere in the body, consciousness has certainly undergone a change, and the environment may have been the cause.

We can do something about that, of course. Exercise is a good way to raise the pH of the body, because it "burns off" some of the drosses accumulated there. Adequate sleep helps in balancing the acids and alkalines in the body. I'm sure that a smile—or any positive emotional response—will change the health and the balance and the pH of the body to an extent.

The conscious mind plays a part, since it can use the power of choice to create new conditions in the functioning portion of the body. And there are medical therapeutic substances—antacids, for instance—that can be used.

Some years ago, when Gladys and I were at Virginia Beach attending a meeting, we were about to go to bed when there was a knock at the door. Someone was having physical difficulty. It was a couple who had a wee baby with a fever. She had been coughing and was restless and wouldn't go to sleep. It was late; the parents had no medicine and wanted to know what to do.

We had with us only Atomidine, Glycothymoline, and castor oil. We chose the Glycothymoline because we knew it would alkalinize the baby's system so that its natural recuperative powers might be restored. We told the parents to give her about five drops of the Glyco in water every three hours.

The baby took one dose and went to sleep very quickly. She awakened once during the night, took another five drops of the Glycothymoline, and slept the rest of the night. In the morning, she was free of fever and cough, and remained that way the rest of the week.

It doesn't take many experiences like this to convince a seeking mind that the body can be benefited simply by being alkalinized to a degree, for it has the ability to defend itself without help if the immune system is given a chance.

7

Exercise
and Meditation

EVERY MORNING DURING THE Temple Beautiful Program, we arise early in the morning, dressed for exercise. Exercises can take many forms, and at the Oak House, they are structured to teach each person that he or she can create a regular exercise program to use at home. Often exercises must be tailored to the individual's physical capabilities at the time. In one program, for example, we had a twenty-three-year-old woman, three weeks postsurgery for a cancer of the ovary, who could not do the same exercises that a seventy-year-old woman with no obvious physical difficulties could do. So we have to adjust to individuals.

The most important thing about exercise is *doing* it! Throughout the world a multitude of ways to exercise the muscles and tendons and joints of the body have been developed. No method, however, is worth anything unless one practices it.

One of the important lessons I learned from my work with the Cayce material is that the body has consciousness that can destroy the effects of an exercise program—no matter what it is. That is, when you start a regular program, then give it up, the body rebels. You may be worse off then than you were when you felt bad and wanted to start exercising.

We advise those who come to one of our progra
tine of exercises that they know they will be able
without fail. It doesn't matter how gingerly you c
that first day—do it and keep on doing it every da
your workout as you go along, if you feel it is OK. But don't be too
ambitious to begin with; that can just bring trouble.

Generally speaking, the best exercises for the entire body are
walking, bicycling, and swimming. Perhaps it's because most of the
body muscles are thoroughly exercised in a coordinated manner in
each of these activities. Most people can do at least one of these at
home if they wish. We recommend doing one of these if possible every
day. If that's not possible for some of our participants, we show them
exercises that can be done indoors. These are designed to keep the
spine flexible, for when this is done, the neurological pathways are
healthier and the communication within the body is more complete.
This always makes for a healthier life and undoubtedly prolongs life
at the same time.

The first exercise is called the "big swing" by some and is done by
standing tall with the feet about 12 to 18 inches apart, whatever feels
most comfortable. Then, starting with arms extended straight out to
the sides from the shoulders, rotate as far to the right as possible,
then rotate to the left as far as possible. Repeat this ten to twenty-five
times, whatever your body currently dictates, but do it *every* day
thereafter. When you do the big swing, let your head rotate almost
ahead of your arms as you swing. That will make the twist from the
top of the spine to the coccyx most effective.

The second exercise is designed to bend the vertebrae in both
directions laterally, from side to side. So, once again, with your feet
12 to 18 inches apart, stand straight, with your hands and arms down
at your sides. First, bend laterally (do *not* twist) to the right, with
your head leading the way. Don't twist the head, and keep facing
forward. When you have bent to that side as far as you can, straighten
up and bend in the same manner to the left. Repeat this exercise the
same number of times you did the big swing, and you are ready for
number three. First, though, please recognize that the first exercise
tended to rotate the vertebrae on each other, while the second simply

ent the whole column laterally with no twisting. Both exercises are designed to make the body more flexible—especially the spinal column. Remember that the spine is supported and limited by the muscles, ligaments, and tendons alongside the column of vertebrae. These are being stretched and moved and stimulated all the time the exercise is going on.

At the same time, bits of calcium that may have been built up on portions of the spine can be gradually dissipated—worn off, one might say. This should not be thought of as being unusual, since it was the inactivity of the same structures that allowed the body to manufacture that material where it is right now. Why not let the body remove it?

The third of the trio is what you would expect. Again take the same stance with feet spread apart, this time with hands and arms reaching for the sky. Then bend first straight forward and touch your fingertips to your toes. Then straighten up once more and bend carefully just as far backward as you can (not too far), with your arms still straight above your head. Repeat this movement the same number of times as you did the other two, and you've finished the "Big Three."

These three exercises will give your spine, from top to bottom, a life-lengthening workout that can do nothing but good for your entire body. It's good to think of this each time you do the exercises. But do be careful in setting up how many of these repetitions you really should do to start with—don't be overenthusiastic about it. No one is keeping score. You are simply improving your body and making for your meditations and prayers a better temple in which to meet the Christ presence.

There are other exercises that might be done as part of a program. One is a head and neck exercise that we use to prepare for meditation. That comes a bit later. Some of our Temple Beautiful group may take a couple of laps around the backyard; others may not. And there are opportunities in the early evening after dinner to go for a walk. Some prefer to walk in the early morning. But people are different and exercises are different.

We have had people in the program who prefer to do tai chi or yoga. We teach the exercises that are part of the Cayce concepts, not that there is anything wrong with other means or methods of exercise.

Right after exercise is a good time to drink a large glass of water. It is cleansing to the system and part of the regimen to drink eight glasses of water daily. Water is best taken before or after meals, not with the meal.

A Cayce recommendation I like is to Work a while after breakfast; then after lunch, rest a while; and after dinner, walk a mile.

Meditation as a Healing Force

Moving from physical movement, as in exercising, to a quiet environment and a stillness of the body allows one to relax and take part in a journey inward. In our program, the relaxation does not come all at once, for there is talk and laughter and settling down into a place and position that is comfortable. Gradually, however, everyone is ready to begin meditation. Then the music starts, and preparations for entry into the meditative state are begun.

Some in the group have never meditated before in their lives. They don't actually know what is expected in meditation or what happens or just what the purpose is of sitting quietly with eyes closed. This is not unusual. Ten years ago, when a television interviewer asked me to explain meditation, I looked at that big television camera, gulped once, and changed the subject. Meditation was not common then, and many thought only people from Indians and "kooks" did it. Today things are different, and I would have no trouble explaining it on television and demonstrating it.

Meditation can be defined as a process of quieting the body, then the mind, holding an affirmation in the mind's eye, and attuning the physical and mental self to its spiritual Source. It is not looking for a revelation, and it is not prayer. One of my favorite people, Elsie Sechrist, says prayer is talking to God—meditation is listening to God.

ir group gets comfortable with the process of meditating, e to sit on the floor in something like a yoga posture; others sit in a chair. We have had some who actually lie on their backs to meditate. What I emphasize is what Edgar Cayce said—sit or take a position where your spine is straight, and if you are sitting in a chair, have your feet flat on the floor. It helps some to take off their shoes and to sit with arms on their lap, with palms upward.

Always, it helps to sit with eyes closed from the start of the preparation exercises to the end of the meditation. This helps to keep the outside world more on the outside while we attempt to probe the inner self.

After everyone has quieted down, we start the music—music that quiets the consciousness and is in one way or another very beautiful. Then we do two easy exercises to prepare us for meditation. The first is the head-and-neck exercise. It is a movement much like the Big Three described earlier, but involving only the head and neck.

First, bend the head forward without moving the body, your chin nearly touching your chest. Return to an upright position. Repeat three times; then bend backward and upright three times. Then bend to the right three times and to the left three times. Then drop the head forward again and move it around to the right, to the rear, to the left, rotating in a full circle three times. Then reverse the rotation to the left in the same manner three times.

Cayce did not give specific physiological reasons for doing this exercise, indicating only that it is a cleansing procedure. But there are activities that go on in the physiology of the body when these movements are being made. For one thing, it stimulates the superior cervical ganglion (cluster of nerve cells) of the sympathetic chain of ganglia, which is the only neurological connection in the body to the pineal gland. The pineal, often called the third eye, is located in the midline directly under the brain. It is the only gland that responds with hormonal activity to that portion of daylight that penetrates the bony skull from the outside world. We understand that X rays can penetrate the body to create an X-ray film and show up tumors or abnormalities; however, we don't often consider the reality that ordinary daylight has some of those same abilities.

The pineal, the highest of the seven spiritual/glandular centers geographically, is thought to be the point at which the mystical marriage takes place when one experiences light during meditation. That is where the divine energy meets the creative energy raised in deep meditation, creating the experience of light. Many enlightened individuals have had such experiences, people like Paul on the road to Damascus, Emanuel Swedenborg, and others, according to Dr. Richard M. Bucke in *Cosmic Consciousness.*

Balancing or clearing the pineal or its attachments is one of the objectives of the head-and-neck exercise. The simple relaxation that comes from this exercise is beneficial too.

After the head-and-neck exercise, we do a special breathing exercise. First, using the left index finger, hold the left nostril closed and inhale through the right nostril, then exhale through the mouth. Do this three times. Then hold the right nostril closed while inhaling through the left nostril, but this time you exhale through the right nostril while the left nostril is held closed. This breathing is done likewise three times.

In India breathing exercises have long played an important part during meditation. But is there a physiological reason for it? I think so. The nerves in the roof of the nasal passages on each side lead directly to the brain. In view of recent findings about the different functions of the two sides of the brain, I think it is only reasonable to think that there is indeed something happening in the neurological system when such a breathing exercise is done.

Cayce suggested that we breathe in purity and exhale those things that need to be released. It is a cleansing, which is appropriate if we enter the state of meditation to meet the Creator in our own Temple of the Living God.

After completing these two exercises, we sit in the quietness, relaxed by the music. Whoever leads the meditation reads an inspirational passage. We select from the Cayce readings something that is applicable to everyone who has ears to hear. Then, from the Bible, we read selections from the fourteenth, fifteenth, sixteenth, and seventeenth chapters of the book of John. These were special words, Cayce indicated, for they were speaking to everyone who would be willing to believe. You may choose other inspirational readings to focus your mind.

This completed, the leader reads an affirmation found in *A Search for God*, the book that is used in the worldwide A.R.E. study group program. The affirmation for the first chapter is:

> Not my will, but thine O Lord, be done in me and through me. May I ever be a channel of blessing, today, now, to those that I contact in every way. Let my going in, my coming out, be in accord with that thou would have me do, and, as the call comes, here am I, send me, use me.

We then enter into the silence to meditate. This lasts ten to fifteen minutes. In meditation, there is an energy that moves up the spine, along the double chain of sympathetic ganglia, starting from the lowest of the spiritual centers, and rising to the pineal, then to the pituitary. Even though it is only an "erg" (as Cayce called it) of energy that makes its way up the spine, when it reaches the pituitary it spills over and, while others are being prayed for, cleanses the body and brings healing. Perhaps not much healing, to be sure, but I am convinced that it is a fact that we must—all of us—sooner or later begin to meditate if we are to reach the goal of oneness with the Creative Force that has been promised. Meditation is followed by praying for others, then saying the Lord's Prayer together.

Then we have our morning hugs. Everyone in the group gets hugged by every other member. The four daily hugs needed for survival are passed in a hurry; the eight for maintenance come immediately afterward; and the twelve for growth get our day started the right way.

Down through history, a tradition has developed about seven spiritual centers or energy points in the human body having great significance. The Eastern religions call them chakras, or spinning wheels of energy. In the West, psychics have seen them as inverted vortices of energy. In a sense, they bear on different endocrine centers in the body.

Cayce's information parallels this latter view. He explains them as points of energy transfer, perhaps where some universal energy enters the body. It is not entirely clear to me whether energy goes in or goes out—perhaps it moves in both directions—but the energies are there, and there seems to be a direct relationship between these spiritual centers and the endocrine glands.

The location of these spiritual centers is associated with the glands. (See chart, The Endocrine Glands.) If you looked at a profile of the human body, you'd note that if connected by a single line, the glandular centers form a shepherd's crook. The pineal is at the top of the curve and the pituitary at the end of the curve. Though the crook's curve is not so great in the body, it is still there. The shepherd's staff has been regarded as the symbol of the seven spiritual centers for centuries.

Another symbol of the seven centers is the pyramid. Standing on top of the pyramid, one can look down four sides to the ground. These are the so-called four lower centers. Standing on the ground and looking at one face of the pyramid, one sees three sides to this triangular face with the point reaching up to the heavens. These are the three higher centers, those keeping us in touch with our heritage.

The spiritual centers each have their own energy patterns. Each of these energies is associated with the feelings and the nature and purpose of the glandular structure itself. Those who see auras might see the energy vortices.

The gonads, which supply the ovum in the female and the sperm in the male, from which life issues, are considered the source of energy, in a sense. The gonads' energy moves upward in meditation. The powers of creativity, whether in procreation or in the arts, music, speaking, writing, acting, or any other creative effort, always involve these glands as the prime movers.

The adrenal gland is our fight-or-flight instrument. It gives us the capacity to meet emergencies. It is connected neurologically with the solar plexus, and together they provide the major force in directing and activating the sympathetic portion of the autonomic nervous system. To give impetus to the body in an emergency, the adrenals (located like little caps over each kidney) first send out shock waves of

The Endocrine Glands

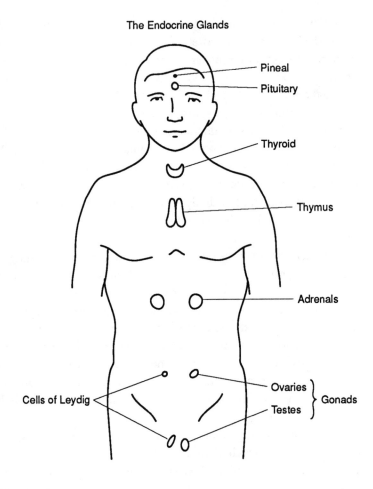

consciousness throughout the body when an emergency arises—be it a lion walking up the hall or a "loved one" threatening to strike you. These neurological messages are transmitted instantaneously. This shuts down the other portion of the autonomic to a large degree. All extraneous—and important digestive—functions are set aside in preparation for action. If action does not come about, then the food, if there is any in the stomach, just lies there and becomes indigestible.

Following the electrical information, the adrenals put out into the bloodstream a ready supply of adrenalin to support the action that is called for. After that, cortisone is released, which gives more long-term support for the proposed action. The action is released energy, which can be constructive or destructive. For example, it has been known for a father, seeing his child pinned under a beam or even a car, to call on that energy and lift weights that he could never lift again. This is constructive use. The destructive use is calling on that energy to harm another person or do something in opposition to one's innermost desires.

Anger and fear both come from these same glands, and have a great deal to do with the creation of illness, with dis-ease or disease. Purification of all these glands comes about through meditation. Thus the fear and the uncalled-for anger can be removed to some extent.

Within the adrenals and the gonads are the cells of Leydig. They provide the body either estrogen or testosterone, which have the prime function of making us either female or male. There is an opportunity for choice as the energy then moves upward, for the movement may be directly upward, or may perhaps start a circle through the adrenals and the thymus and back down—which is commonly called the wheel of karma. It is in this area that one experiences temptation in the earth domain.

The thymus gland, the fourth of the spiritual/glandular centers, is considered the director and moving force of the immune system. It sends out colonies of cells during the early months of life to set up lymphatic centers throughout the body, and even during the later years of life, it fulfills a function of defense that has only been recognized in the past two decades.

In the emotional makeup of individuals, the thymus is recognized as the heart or the love center. It is interesting to me that the thymus gland actually begins as part of the thyroid, in its embryological development, then migrates down out of the heavens (symbolically) and into the earth, and becomes a symbol of love in the affairs of the human being. It is symbolized by the eagle, too, which flies high in the heavens, but really is bound to the earth and part of it; it still has its nest. But the emotions of pity and warmth, of jealousy and giving, of tenderness and love all are found in this center. Again, it is for better or worse that this portion of our bodies is activated.

Whereas the thymus is the eagle, the gonads are seen as the calf or the bull, the cells of Leydig as the androgynous human, and the adrenals as the lion. The thyroid, pineal, and pituitary are not symbolized by beasts, since they are really of the heavens, and the beasts do not reside there. The thyroid is the symbol of will or choice; the pineal is the inner eye; and the pituitary is the master gland, or the cup that is filled. Much has been written about these seven glandular/spiritual centers by those who have studied this aspect of the Cayce readings.

The thyroid gland, situated just above the line of the shoulders, is instrumental as the site of the power of choice or the will. Its hormonal activity is responsible for either the laxity found in not having the will power to avoid food, for example, or for inspiring activity in worthwhile ventures. One who has avoided using his or her will power over several incarnations will find it difficult to accomplish things this time around because of the habit structures that have been created in the thyroid and the unconscious mind.

The pineal, on the other hand, controls the cycles in the body. It is a regulator of the body, in addition to being what we think of as the inner eye, the point where the higher forces reach down and touch the energy that has been raised in meditation and thus create light.

The most important gland, probably, is the pituitary. It is the master of all the other six. Together with the others, the pituitary creates a pattern of energy movement in the body that helps to provide that unique balance of energies that makes each individual different from any other on the face of the earth.

Most of the time, those who are just beginning meditation are too self-conscious to experience the quietness inside or to have any so-called experiences during the period. Their minds are much too busy trying to quiet down the conscious mind, which won't hold still no matter what they do. But with regular meditation, this problem is gradually solved, and occasionally the experience of the "light" will suddenly come into their consciousness, and their lives will be changed in a remarkable manner.

All this, of course, contributes to healing. It is part of what I call Edgar Cayce's medicine for today. When cleansing and spiritual growth come about, things that have bound one to an illness are released, and the body begins to change; there comes to the functioning of the body a better balance, a better coordination of the body parts. Choice has created change in the former patterns that brought the disease into being.

8

Medical Guidance

BECAUSE OF MY COMMITMENT to a different approach to the practice of medicine, someone whom I've never met before asks the inevitable question—"What kind of doctor are you?" My immediate answer is, "I'm a *good* doctor." With a smile, I then clarify their confusion at my answer and give the background in medicine that it's been my privilege to experience this lifetime.

But I would not take back my first answer. I am a good doctor. I am not a surgeon, nor do I any longer assist at surgery. I no longer deliver babies, although I have, and under very primitive conditions in Kentucky early in my career. I am not an orthopedist, nor am I a neurologist, an endocrinologist, a pediatrician, an internist, a dermatologist—but I am a general practitioner turned family physician with my interests and expertise developed in the field of helping individuals return their bodies to normal.

Because of the kind of work we do at the Clinic, our special residential programs become filled with people who have gone to the Mayo Clinic, the Cleveland Clinic, and other well-known centers, as well as having consulted many other physicians. They come to us with diagnoses already made, so we have no need to be experts in the conventional methods of diagnosis. There are physicians in our community whom we call on for needs we cannot fill.

But each person who enters a Temple Beautiful Program receives a full, complete physical examination, and we elicit an extensive history from each. The careful taking of a medical history has long been recognized by the profession as essential in arriving at the proper diagnosis, but our history extends beyond what is usually taken. We obtain the past history, the story of surgery and traumatic events of the body, the family history, and the systems review.

We find out, from the story of their present illness, just what has been happening in our patients' lives. We find out how many marriages they have had and the details of the emotions involved in each one. What about their childhood experiences? Did their parents provide a loving environment, or was it filled with fear because of substance abuse? Were they reprimanded because they were "no good"? Were they sexually abused? Questions like that let them know that we are really interested in putting together the information so as to deal with the etiology behind the etiology of the problem they are currently working with. For all illnesses have a cause that is found somewhere in the relationship between body, mind, and spirit—and in what the individual has been doing relative to that which he or she has chosen as the ideal in life.

Laboratory tests are taken. There are always certain groups of tests that help us understand best what is going on physiologically in the body at the time, but others that are pertinent for specific problems are also ordered. We often do a five-hour glucose tolerance test to identify those who have hypoglycemia, which is truly a problem often unrecognized in conventional medical care and cannot be diagnosed without such extensive blood tests. After the first blood test is taken with the patient fasting, the patient is given a drink containing 100 grams of glucose. Then, during the subsequent five hours, the blood sugar level will often drop 20, 30, or 40 points below the average norm for fasting blood sugar. This is true hypoglycemia.

The symptoms experienced during this time often mirror what the patient who is hypoglycemic experiences three or four hours after eating something very sweet. The patient may be listless or tired, nauseated, sick, and very sleepy. Treatment during the test—if the patient is quite ill—is to administer orange juice or a piece of fruit. When the diagnosis is established, a diet is instituted that allows a piece of cold chicken or protein tablets or fruit, or even a glass of milk, between meals. And the patient is told to avoid sugars and heavy starches and desserts. In addition, a course of therapy is designed that will strengthen the adrenal glands, which are thought to be one of the causative factors, and keep the fasting blood sugar at normal levels.

We often suspect systemic candidiasis—a yeast infection throughout the body from the patient's history of having taken excessive amounts of hormones or antibiotics. The yeast then overgrows in the intestinal tract and in the vagina. The diagnosis is established by use of a questionnaire that was developed originally by Dr. William G. Crook (*The Yeast Connection*) and sometimes by obtaining a blood test to demonstrate the body's response to the presence of the yeast. When the yeast cells have invaded the tissues of the body, the host becomes chronically ill and has usually seen many physicians for a multitude of complaints without receiving a definitive diagnosis. When we have made the diagnosis satisfactorily, we use a special diet that eliminates any foods that yeast would normally feed upon. And most often we prescribe an antifungal agent over a long period of time to rid the body of the yeast.

During that time, also, we give treatments that are designed to enhance the immune system so that the body can aid in overcoming the infection.

We do not routinely order X rays, for these more extensive tests often are done elsewhere before the patient arrives at our clinic. But we do take those tests that tell us how the physiology of the body is doing and what it is we are dealing with.

We will often talk about life and death, always expressing it as a true continuum. Many of our patients have had a near-death experience. Books have been written about this remarkable event, which seems to be telling us not only that there is life beyond this one, but that it is truly more like our natural habitat. If we *are* created in God's image, then the spiritual realm *would* be our natural place of existence.

The *American Journal of Diseases of Children* published an article in October 1983 by a pediatrician, Melvin Morse, who wanted to "make pediatricians aware that near-death experiences can occur in children as well as adults" and to stress that the children "may benefit from counseling concerning such experiences." One child told interviewers that the first memory of her near-drowning was being in the water. She said "I was dead. Then I was in a tunnel and I was scared. I couldn't walk." Then she told how the tunnel became bright after a tall, blond woman named Elizabeth appeared, and together they walked to heaven. She said that "heaven was fun. . . . It was bright and there were lots of flowers."

She described a border around heaven beyond which she could not see, and said she met many people, including her dead grandparents, her dead maternal aunt, and Heather and Melissa, two adults waiting to be reborn. Then she met the "heavenly Father and Jesus," who asked her if she wanted to return to earth. She replied, "No." Elizabeth then asked the girl if she wanted to see her mother, who was still living. She said yes and wakened once again in the hospital, where she had been taken.

This takes some of the onus off the idea of dying, doesn't it? It also helps the ailing person to believe that life truly is a continuous thing, and one is here for a deeper purpose than just being healed of what we call illness.

These approaches help anyone to ease the fear of dying, in the first place, and also to become more aware of why we are here and what we are doing about it. Some of those who are part of our programs are very near the time when they will take the next step in the cycle of reincarnation and be born into the next dimension. Others, like the little girl, still have something burning inside of them that they want to do, people they want to be in contact with. They simply are not yet ready to move on.

When one considers, however, that birth and death are the entry and exit each of us *must* take in order to experience this earth-life, neither should be looked at with fear. We need to welcome a newborn entity into this dimension just as other souls welcome those who are born into the spiritual realm. Our conversation about life and death with our patients is as matter-of-fact as the discussion of their diet or their tendency toward constipation.

When we speak so easily of life beyond death, and of this earth experience being an opportunity for soul growth, then it behooves us to step back a bit and look at the source of the information we are using. There are thousands today who are giving psychic information on healing. They get their information from sources that are beyond the conscious mind. How does it all fit in with the present scheme of things in the world of healing and medicine? Since the work we have been doing with the A.R.E. Clinic deals specifically with psychic information as given by Edgar Cayce, this question seems appropriate.

Cayce was once asked, "Where does this information come from? What is its source?" He answered, "Universal Forces." As I understand that, in the light of what he said at other times, Cayce had to have spent earlier lifetimes following divine principles in order to be able to tap the universal sources of information this time around. This is an important principle to remember when looking at other psychics. How are they living their lives? Are they committed to the principle of serving their fellow human beings? Or does their psychic ability disguise their use of it to gain recognition as one who is gifted and spiritually advanced?

I tell our patients that everyone is psychic, since psychic is "of the soul." Everyone dreams, everyone has hunches and imagination, all of which are psychic qualities. Yet we are not all psychic enough to easily recognize it. Some express their soul quality through music, some through art or sculpturing or building, others by writing.

Occasionally, I'll read some of the things I've written and say to myself with a bit of surprise, "That's really not bad at all! How did I do that?" Well, I know that when I sit down at my typewriter, I ask that the God part of myself manifest as those thoughts and words that will be helpful to others and touch their hearts and souls so there will come changes in consciousness for the better in all who read my

words. My thoughts are expressed better in writing than I could ev[e]
say them. Others who are expressing their soul selves do it differently.
Each one is in attunement with what is sometimes called the higher
self, or the Christ consciousness within.

As patients come to understand some of these concepts, they begin to be a bit in awe of themselves. At the same time, however, they
are starting the process of seeing themselves in a new light and understanding themselves better as having that potential that allows
their bodies to resume the natural estate: health. That is helpful.

It's best not to be in a hurry to increase our psychic ability but to
use what we *do* have creatively and helpfully for others and for ourselves. Cayce, in a reading for an intense individual with high aspirations, was asked how he could gain access to omnipotence, omni-
science, and omnipresence. Cayce encouraged taking the path of soul
growth step by step and not overevaluating where our minds can take
us when our bodily actions do not yet measure up. He said:

> This ability—to speak, to apply, to be present in Omnipresence—is
> attained by having fully, completely met all that has been error in the
> experience of the body, mind and soul in the earth experience. Not that
> this is not attainable, but one grows to that consciousness in
> the application of the faith in and the consciousness of being at-one
> with the divine that is within. This may not then be given as yet.
> (no. 2533–8)

This same man asked a question later on in the same reading
about the "Hidden Way." Perhaps he referred to a mystical course of
action that is to be fashioned in the material world. The answer gives
more insight to anyone seeking to be of service in the healing profes-
sions, whether doctor or patient:

> For as was given so oft, this is found within. For thy body is indeed the
> pattern of the heavenly body, yet it only grows to same, as it grows away
> from same; though it may be within the three-dimensional realm. This
> is the Hidden Way. For as the entity uses, never abuses but uses self in
> service, it finds the Way. For who is the greater among you? "He that is
> the servant of all." Who would know the Hidden Way? They who seek
> to do His biddings alone. (no. 2533–8)

use whatever psychic ability one may be able to
, it is well to remember that we are dealing with
that we call life, which is monitored, directed,
by a quality called will. And the will of an individual
is greater than any other power. Each individual has the will power,
even, to deny the creative forces. As Cayce put it:

> . . . the will of a soul, of a body, is supreme—even as to whether it
> makes of itself a channel for the spiritual influences in its experience or
> for the selfish desires of its own body and its aggrandizing of those
> influences. (no. 2533–8)

Cayce said that about 80 percent of the time the results are determined by what a body does with its opportunities. Perhaps this is
why he said that nothing happens by chance. I suspect healing of the
body really does depend to a great extent on chance—what the patient decides to do with this opportunity at this time, in relation to
what the patient knows deep within is his or her divine destiny.

We use a variety of methods of healing the body at the Clinic—
medicine, osteopathy, chiropractic, massage therapy, acupuncture,
acupressure, transcutaneous electrotherapy, electromagnetic field
therapy, patterning, biofeedback training, autogenic exercises, visualization, and nutrition, to mention some—but each method falls
under a banner of oneness that we call an ideal. All healing is really
from one Source, so why be concerned about the method? As Cayce
put it, whether the practitioner prescribes a drug or a spinal
adjustment,

> the healing comes from within. Not by the method does the healing
> come, though the consciousness of the individual may be such that this
> or that method *is* the one that is more effective in the individual case in
> arousing the forces from within. But methods are not ideals. The *ideal*
> must be kept in the proper source. (no. 969–1)

One of the unconventional methods that we use effectively to
combat jetlag came to us originally from a lovely Indian physician
about ten years ago. When travelers arrive at the Clinic after a trans-

continental plane trip, we suggest they bathe that night in a tub of tepid water to which has been added one cup of epsom salts and one cup of baking soda. While in the tub, they massage the right side of their body with their right hand and the left side with the left hand, making sure that the arms and legs on both sides stay in their own territory and do not cross the midline of the body. After 10–15 minutes, they dry off, again without crossing extremities. It's difficult, but it can be done. Then they are to go to bed for the night. When they arise, no jet lag.

This treatment might well have come from the Cayce readings, for he gave credence to energies that involved the four extremities and the umbilicus, describing a flow of energy in the human body that moves in the shape of a figure eight, crossing at the umbilicus, stating that this was an important energy activity.

Our theory is that the solution in the bathtub provides an electromagnetic field that impacts the figure-eight flow of energy and normalizes the controls of the cycles of the body found in the pineal gland. Whether the theory is ever proved or disproved, patients do benefit from the bath. My wife and I always use it when traveling, carrying a plastic bag of the mixture in our suitcases. Friends and patients who've tried it report favorable results. A doctor from Tasmania said that he and his wife both tried it. "I found one had to concentrate while drying off, but . . . we both slept well and did not have that awful jet lag."

A woman who had a fifteen-hour flight from Panama to Germany, arriving at 5:00 P.M., said she took along her packet of epsom salts and sodium bicarbonate and got in the tub about 7:00 P.M. "I soaked for twenty minutes (nearly fell asleep) and was very careful not to cross either my arms or my legs over my body. I went to bed shortly thereafter and slept my normal eight hours and got up in the morning ready for breakfast as though I had been living here all my life."

This method of bringing health to the body may not seem important, although it certainly is to the sufferer of jet lag, but it shows one "method" of healing. Though it may have originated as folk medicine from India, I would put it in the category of energy medicine, for the electromagnetic field generated impacts body energies, having a normalizing effect on the traveler's physiology.

Many of our patients receive not one but several different methods of healing. One man who came to the Clinic at the insistence of his son, accompanied by his wife, was almost doubled over in pain. He had undergone prostate surgery six weeks earlier and had been sleeping very little since. He had lost considerable weight and required assistance in order to walk. He could not manage more than fifteen or twenty steps before needing to sit down. He was miserable. He said he came to the program "praying for a miracle."

When he left, his color was one of health; he stood up straight; his pain was gone; he was sleeping well; his sense of humor had returned; and he reported, "I received the miracle I was praying for!" How was this achieved in seventeen days? Massages, manipulations, prayers, visualizations, guided imageries, autogenic exercises, biofeedback training, acuscope treatments, meditation, and guidance through dreams—these spelled the difference and created a balance of the body functions. They are all different methods, aren't they? The awakened consciousness certainly plays the major part in recovery.

9

Assimilation
and Elimination

In our approach to healing the human body, we find common sense to be a tremendous aid. In my medical school training, very little attention was given to the subject of diet and nutrition. True, there were diets given for different diseases sometimes, but what happens physiologically when a body is either overfed or underfed was a subject not touched upon.

It was as if the process of assimilation was only of passing interest. Elimination, of course, drew even less attention, for everyone eliminates, don't they?

Common sense dictates, however, that the entire body is made up, physically, of what is taken by mouth, either food or life-giving air (unless one is in a critical care center being given intravenous feedings). Common sense also tells us that we will die if the waste products of our metabolism are not removed from the body in some manner. Elimination occurs mainly from the kidneys and from the liver and intestinal tract. The skin and the lungs do their part too, but the first two provide the most relief.

Cayce identified human waste products as used and refused forces. He saw food as a force of building within the body. What is left over from the building plus the breakdown of body cells become the "used" forces. If one eats more than is needed, the body will refuse to assimilate it, and it then becomes a "refused force."

Some years ago, I was called to see an elderly woman who was constipated. Examination showed that she either had impacted feces or a pathological bowel obstruction. Although very sick, she refused to be hospitalized. If she was going to die, she said, it would be right there in her home.

I knew that I could not force her into the hospital, nor, really, should I do so. I recommended that she put a castor oil pack without the heating pad on her abdomen, which was greatly distended. I suggested she take nothing by mouth but ice chips. This was to keep her from overloading her stomach and possibly vomiting. The next morning she was feeling much better, but she continued taking only ice chips. The second morning, with the pack still in place, she was markedly improved. Her abdomen was almost flat, and she felt well enough to watch television again. I had her use a mild laxative suppository on the third day, and she had a normal bowel movement. Her sense of humor had returned, and she was back to normal physically. Apparently, the castor oil pack had relieved the obstruction to the extent that other activities within her body could return to normal. Thus, the distention was relieved, and she finally had a normal bowel movement.

Assimilation is often confused with digestion. These are two distinct functions. Digestion is performed by the salivary juices in the mouth and the acids, enzymes, and digestive substances from the stomach, the pancreas, the gall bladder and liver, and probably the lining of the small intestine. Each contributes to the digestive process, which breaks down the food in this manner so that the next step, assimilation, can take place. During assimilation the various food substances that have been worked on by all these internal glands and their products are now in a form that can be absorbed into the intestinal walls and thence, by the lymphatics or blood supply, carried to the liver and to the rest of the body. This distribution system allows the tissues of the body to rebuild and form new cells. It is not a simple procedure, but these broken-down molecules of foods are the energies or forces that Cayce calls the building blocks of the human body.

Coordination between the functions of assimilation and elimination is necessary to life itself. We cannot expect normal health when foods are not being assimilated. The story I told earlier of the little girl who fell and paralyzed her solar plexus with resultant "malabsorption syndrome" shows what can happen when lack of assimilation occurs. Her further paralysis of the function of elimination (one bowel movement every two weeks) only emphasizes the need for this function to be active. Living a long life, said Cayce, depends on these two functions being "kept nearer normal."

Thus we not only pay attention to the diet of every patient who comes to us, but we want to understand what is going on in the physiology of the eliminations of that person. Eliminations are aided in many ways, as you can see by visiting your neighborhood pharmacy.

One of the most common methods for keeping the eliminations regular is to drink lots of water. We recommend at least eight glasses of water daily, especially for those who have a lot of trouble with constipation. Another way to keep the large intestine normally active is to take a large green salad at noon. The high alkalinity of the meal when nothing else is taken will often correct normally sluggish bowels.

Castor oil packs often relieve a temporary siege of constipation, if used over a period of several days. Also, we have suggested to some of our patients that a dropperful of castor oil taken on the tongue at bedtime will tend to relieve the problem.

Cayce suggested, and we have found from our experience, that keeping on with one cathartic or eliminant is unwise. It is advisable to change from one type of laxative to another occasionally. But it is better to create normal bowel habits. Regularity is aided by exercise, such as walking, a diet that is high in fresh green vegetables, and lots of water daily.

Keep in mind that the body can take in all that is necessary to rebuild itself if it is not hindered by the failure of the eliminations to do their part. I've often thought about the wonderful ability of the body to deliver the food substances to the cells as well as carry off their waste products. It is almost like asking your garbage man to bring along your groceries when he comes by to pick up the trash. The same blood that does the feeding also carries away the waste to the organs of eliminations. We have a wonderful body, don't we?

If the eliminants do not do their job properly, the large bowel, which is the major channel of eliminations, must be cleansed. The kidney does a major part of the work, but the bowel is number one. Cleansing can be done to some extent with enemas taken at home, but colonic irrigations are more extensive and have more far-reaching physiological benefits.

When the colon is irrigated with warm water, first the fecal content is cleared out, and then the water allows a flow of "used and refused" forces to be released from the capillaries of the large intestinal wall into the lumen of the large bowel.

Colon irrigation is thus more effective than a cathartic or laxative is in simply cleansing the large bowel, for a colonic in addition provides a cleansing of the bloodstream. Further, the physical act of filling the bowel with water and then emptying it tends to stimulate the muscular lining of the bowel into more normal activity. Colon irrigations are part of the therapy program of every participant in the Temple Beautiful. This kind of activity (currently done with throwaway sterile equipment) has a beneficial effect that is generally not recognized by the medical profession.

There are, of course, conditions of illness in which colonics should not be administered, but these are really not common and should be recognized without difficulty.

With a good basic diet allowing proper assimilation in the body and with adequate and normal elimination, the stage is really set for the fulfilling of Cayce's prophecy that, with proper assimilation and elimination, one can live as long as one chooses. Unfortunately, good things are never just that simple. But it is an important place from which to begin.

The Liver-Kidney Relationship

Both the liver and the kidneys are dynamic forces in the function of elimination, but the liver is also involved with digestion, since much of the assimilated food particles, as they travel from the walls of the small intestine, next go to the liver.

Furthermore, these two vital organs must be functioning properly for the body's electrical system to work effectively. Cayce refers to them as two poles of electricity in the body, actually giving life to the body. All bodily functions, of course, are driven by electrical energy, so the importance of the liver and kidneys in this context cannot be overestimated. One serves as the negative pole, the other the positive. When electrical disturbances develop, the effect is that of a short circuit, said Cayce. A short circuit causes poisons to be dumped into the system instead of being properly eliminated by these organs. Medical science does not agree with this concept, but that's the picture Cayce painted.

The relationship Cayce sees between the liver and the kidneys as positive and negative poles of the electrical body helps to explain the formation of kidney stones. He told a fifty-six-year-old woman that "accumulations in the kidney itself from conditions where incoordinations between the circulations of liver and kidneys have caused sediments to form, irritations that, as to size and conditions, will require operative measures" (no. 3623–1). And then he said, "We would operate."

In another instance (no. 5137–1) he identified subluxations (i.e., partial dislocations) between the seventh and eighth dorsal vertebrae as the cause of hindrances in the nerve energies going to the activities between the liver and kidneys, which in turn produced trouble in the gallbladder. Apparently the electrical poles were disrupted in their coordination of electrical energies.

Whenever there is a disturbance of eliminations in the human body, toxic forces will be recirculated throughout the body, and sooner or later according to the conditions present, this will cause physical difficulty that creates dis-ease, then eventually a disease of the body, unless corrected somewhere along the way.

10

Manipulation and Massage

EARLY IN OUR CAREERS, Gladys's dad taught us some rudiments of osteopathy. Her parents were both graduates of Kirksville College of Osteopathy. Dr. Andrew Taylor Still, the founder of the discipline, was their teacher. Still understood the body to be a fine mechanism that is controlled in both health and disease by electrical impulses that could be disturbed by pressure on nerves carrying those impulses. Manipulation of the large muscle masses or portions of the body could improve or relieve the condition and thus effect a cure. This is the basis of osteopathy.

We learned a very simple technique to relieve what we clinically call a sacroiliac syndrome. It is not difficult. With the ailing patient lying on a treatment table, face up, we take the leg on the side that is giving the most discomfort and flex it on the thigh. Then, we gently let the flexed extremity rotate laterally to the side, maintaining the flexion. After we have achieved as much of the lateral movement as possible, the knee is held flat, as much as possible, and the leg then extended. It is sometimes amazing how one such treatment will bring a surprised and delighted look to the face of the sufferer, and solve the problem.

We used this technique effectively from the beginning of our practice in Ohio. When we moved to Arizona in 1955 and turned our practice over to another physician, we received a weekly phone call from our successor as he sought advice about each patient. One week he frantically wanted to know, "What in the world did you do for George M?" George's sacroiliac syndrome was bothering him again, and he had come in to get the same treatment we had given him. The new doctor was at a loss to help. Osteopathy, of course, is much more complex than George's treatment. When physicians don't learn how to do manipulations in medical school or later, they simply do not have the skills to help people in a way that sometimes is very necessary.

Gladys's mother and dad, who were medical missionaries in India, used to give each other a general osteopathic treatment once or twice every week. It helped them over a multitude of difficulties while they were in the mission field. And it has been a rich addition to our own armamentarium, especially during the times when we had no access to either an osteopath or a chiropractor. Today, in the Clinic, both are available.

Although the American Medical Association was openly hostile to chiropractic for many years, a number of doctors recognized its value.* An article in the January 23, 1981, issue of the *American Medical News*, "Some MDs Called 'Closet Manipulators,'" reported that many physicians throughout the nation at that time were using manipulative techniques similar to those used by chiropractors but had become "closet manipulators" for fear of being ostracized. An AMA delegate from Washington who testified in a lawsuit by chiropractors against the AMA and other medical organizations said that he had hundreds of patients in common with chiropractors in his community, and that he routinely uses techniques of manipulation in his practice.

The AMA at one time discriminated against osteopaths, criticiz-

---

*Chiropractic is a therapeutic system of adjustment consisting of palpation of the spinal column to ascertain partial dislocations of the vertebrae, followed by spinal adjustment by hand, in order to relieve certain nerve pressure.

ing them as unscientific quacks. It officially reversed its position and accepted them into the medical community more than a decade ago.

When the AMA tried to destroy the chiropractic profession by boycotting the chiropractors, they sued the AMA and won. The AMA could no longer prevent physicians from having professional relationships with chiropractors. That was a positive step, because people need to be free to use the skills of these practitioners.

Cayce sent people to both osteopaths and chiropractors from the early days of this century when he started giving readings. His theory about manipulative techniques and the need for them parallels Dr. Still's writings. (See Gail Cayce, *Osteopathy*.)

In this approach to healing the body, Cayce indicated that osteopathy was the best form of treatment—better than conventional medicine or other methods. Medical research in anatomy and physiology and Cayce's understanding of the body are really very close. We know that there are sympathetic ganglia that exist in a long chain from the neck to the coccyx on either side of the spinal column inside the body cavity. We know too that these are interconnected and that they have a functional relationship to the autonomic activities of the body and also to the brain and spinal cord. Cayce's description parallels that of medical science. In addition, he sees tiny bursas (or sacs) within these ganglia. And these can become congested, or slow in their response to any portion of the system. Cayce paints a picture of each organ and each gland of the system receiving information/impulses from the active mind, from suggestion, from sensory input, and from the environment. This communication then extends to every portion of the human body in its activity. These key centers then may bring about a balance by functioning properly—or an imbalance. And this can happen from food taken internally or from injections or from any human activity.

Cayce said that the science of osteopathy is not merely the working of a certain segment or the cracking of the bones, but instead osteopathic manipulation restores a balance between the sympathetic nervous system and the cerebrospinal. These create coordination and a release of energies through the spine to the rest of the body and at the same time work toward clearing up the problem in the bursa (as he described it) or the osteopathic lesion (as osteopathy describes it), which can often be a cause of illness. As Cayce reminded people, mechanical adjustments, like medicines, "are only correctives—and NATURE or the DIVINE force, does the healing" (no. 1467–9).

To understand fully how an osteopathic lesion may be formed or released, or how a subluxation of vertebra could come about, it would be best to look at some of the texts on osteopathy or chiropractic. Cayce took these things for granted, telling people what was wrong in the spine and how it could be corrected.

Granted that life conditions can bring about such disturbances in one's consciousness that a subluxation is created, then Cayce does better at indicating how the whole body may become involved. He said that any abnormal condition of the body, no matter what it is, sets up a strain and tends to take energy from other portions of the system to correct the strain. The equilibrium is then disturbed, and some portion of the system always suffers as a result of the original problem. "Though the pain may be in the back, the suffering may be in the head, or intestinal system, or in other organs of the system" (no. 5618–9). One must then restore balance through correction of the lesion.

Massaging the Body

In addition to manipulation, Cayce found massage highly therapeutic. Every participant in our Temple Beautiful programs experiences what is called a "massage to music." And it always becomes a truly unique and meaningful life experience.

Stan, a truck driver in his fifties, had developed a cancer of the lung before he came through one of our recent programs. He had been smoking most of his life. The spiritual realities that were apparent to most members of the group were meaningless to him. He was an unbeliever in "all this stuff"—or so he said. He was not a big man, but he was wiry, muscular, probably strong before his illness, and pretty much of a "macho" individual. Stan had not gotten along with his daughter for years and wouldn't show that this really hurt him deeply. It became evident that he needed desperately to forgive his daughter, no matter what the girl had done.

Very early in the nine-day program, Stan had a massage to music. He didn't really want it but couldn't find a good excuse to get out of having it.

These treatments, first designed by Kay Ortmans, who started using them up in the redwoods of California near Santa Cruz, last two to three hours. No oil is used, but the body is kept warm under a sheet. The massage is deep and moves the body, but is never painful.

It's the movement of large muscle groups that stirs up memories of past events—often from past lives. And it is done while classical music is played so that the whole room resounds with the music. The music acts as a bridge between the conscious and the unconscious. But many life experiences are tagged with certain muscle groups, and the combination of the circumstances, the expectations, the music, and the movement bring much that is worthwhile out of the unconscious mind.

Stan didn't realize what he was getting into. He had needs that hadn't yet been met, something to do with his lungs. Within this area lies the thymus, or the heart center. It is here that feelings of remorse, sadness, and hurt are locked into one's consciousness, and this is the area where Stan was hurting.

Things went smoothly on the surface as his therapy began, until Barbara started massaging his chest. Suddenly it was as though a tremendous burst of electrical energy entered his head and went through his body and out through his feet. And they were no longer Barbara's hands massaging his chest; he felt Jesus' hands moving into his chest and working something out. Stan began crying, for he had never really felt that the story of Jesus was actually true. But there was the Master, working on the inside of his chest where all the hurt had been for so many years.

When it ended and he finally stopped the tears, Stan shared part of the story with the rest of the group. For the rest of the week at the Oak House, he tried to relive the experience, to have it happen again. He could not.

On the last full day of the program, some of the group visited our home. In the largest room, which we call the library, we have a chair that Gladys gave me for Father's Day in 1952. It tilts back and is very comfortable. It's been through two generations and five homes but is still almost like new. All of our six kids, when they got sick with the childhood ailments, spent time on that chair. We always figured that if the kids slept there, they would take on those healing "vibes" that gradually developed and get better more quickly.

Stan sat in that chair while everyone was socializing around the house. He leaned back and closed his eyes, and after a little while I saw a few tears trickle down his cheek. I quietly went over and patted them with a tissue and moved the chair a bit to make it more comfortable. Stan stayed there quite a while, then finally got up and joined the rest of us who were nearby chatting.

After a while, someone asked if he'd like to share what had happened. The story unfolded. He told us how he had wanted desperately to relive that experience he had had during the massage to music. He had not been able to, he told us, but when he arrived at our house he wanted to sit down on that chair. Suddenly he felt that same energy moving in his body, pouring out through his feet. The hands of Jesus were not part of this experience, but the feeling was similar.

Stan forgave his daughter. It was probably the end of a hostility that had existed over many lifetimes. The experience also made him aware of the reality of Jesus in his life, something he had never had before. These were the purposes, undoubtedly, that he came to fulfill this lifetime. Several months later he died. Many others were richer because of what he experienced, and shared, and so is his soul, I feel sure. He was but one of many people whose lives have been changed through this unique therapy.

When Erika gives a massage to music, the sounds of Beethoven and Tchaikovsky and the other masters provide a foundation of vibration that allows much opening up of valuable material from the unconscious. Erika calls down the angels and the forces of the heavens to help her—and they do.

In addition to this massage, our therapists provide full-body therapeutic massages. These are fifty-minute treatments, designed to bring balance to the functioning of the human body. Some of our therapists like to play music during this time, and the patient is urged not to talk, so that the body can receive the benefits of massage most effectively.

One receives best by being in a receptive mode. One can hardly hear if one is also talking. Thus asking questions or discussing a problem, no matter what, diminishes the healing benefits of a massage.

When a therapeutic massage is given, it should be understood by both the therapist and the recipient that a massage is always, in addition to a working with the tissues of the body, an actual laying on of hands. Every person affects the individual he or she touches. It is always a giving of healing energy or a taking away. Our therapists understand that they are healing through their touch as well as doing the mechanics of the procedure. If the one receiving a message understands this too, greater benefit will come through being receptive to both physical healing activity as well as what comes through the energy transmitted.

Although even an occasional massage is beneficial, I always try to remind people of the benefits to be gained through regular massage. I've heard—although I have no idea whether it is true or not—that Bob Hope has a massage every day. Something he is doing, whether it's the joy he spreads in other people's lives or a daily massage or whatever, seems to be making him look younger to me every time I see him on television. Ten or fifteen years ago, he looked eighty—now he looks ten years younger, seventy, going on forty-five.

One time, many years ago, my friend Dr. Harold Reilly (who was sent patients in the Cayce readings for treatments hundreds of times) gave me an answer I've quoted to anyone who asks me, "How frequently should I get a massage?" The answer: "The frequency of massages is determined totally by the size of the pocketbook." An hour's time with a trained therapist does not come for nothing, so many patients looking for help have to evaluate what their individual body needs in the way of massage, and follow that guidance, as well as their pocketbook.

What benefits does a body receive from massage? If you were to draw your right hand gently and caringly from the left wrist up to the shoulder, you would, first of all, feel better because of the loving manner in which you treated your left arm. That's the love factor. You would also benefit—and this may be part of the "feeling better"—from the millions of impulses to the cerebrospinal nervous system that were generated in the massage you just completed. Although it involves just your left arm, there were also other millions of messages given to the autonomic nervous system, which controls the entire functioning of the life-support systems and organs.

This explains why it is important that therapists be in a giving, loving mode while they perform a massage—and why it is perhaps doubly important that the patient be receptive to all that the massage can bring in the way of healing to his or her body.

All these functions can be understood to be going on during a massage. But Cayce saw a rather specific thing happening in the massage that was given to an eighteen-year-old boy (no. 2456–4) who had acute leukemia. He noted that some of the ganglia along the spine were either lax in their function or tight—allowing some organs to receive too many impulses and others too few. In this boy, massages would not only aid the circulation through various portions of the body but also aid the ganglia to receive nerve impulses more accurately and dispense them in a more balanced manner.

A massage could be understood to be bringing a balancing effect to the entire organism of the human body. It's like a gentle rain of impulses causing the body to start coordinating in a more constructive manner. It's also like the quieting effect on a group of one person's gentle love.

Music that is creative, not destructive, is often helpful during a massage, but both the therapist and the patient must agree on it. The patient may prefer a period of quiet. In that case, quiet is best.

One part of the body may need special attention. Maybe it is the low back that has been ailing the most, or the shoulder or neck or perhaps the abdomen. Cayce gave numerous suggestions about the specifics of massage, where it would be best to concentrate attention. The full study of the readings has not yet been done, although Mary

Alice Duncan, a registered physical therapist, wrote an article in the January 1970 *A.R.E. Journal* about massage as it was described in the Cayce readings.

Cayce suggested that a very specific massage to the feet was often very important. He said, "massage more in the bursa of the feet, as under the toe, in the instep and in the heel" (no. 2778–6). This would cause some twitching later on of the calves and perhaps under the knees and in the thighs, but works to reestablish proper communication between the lower limbs and the origin of the sciatic nerves, which is in the lower part of the back. In a sense, the nerves of the ends of the sciatics would be enlivened or stimulated to normal function.

Most often, massages are given to increase the lymphatic flow toward the heart, in a sense. Exercise such as walking does this, since the entire lymph circulation has valves and muscular walls that move the lymph toward its destination. These muscles are very, very fine, but they are there.

Sometimes, Cayce suggested massage to be directed away from the brain. This was particularly true for a person who has had a stroke. The brain is the center of an effort on the part of the body to repair, and it may already be congested with circulation and the immune system's efforts to repair. In other cases, a massage was suggested to aid nerve functioning—and this may be part of the reason Cayce suggested to massage away from the brain, to bring normal impulses down to the malfunctioning nervous system on the affected side of the body.

Occasionally, Cayce suggested using a vibrator. For indigestion, he instructed (no. 389–9) to use the vibrator "over the whole of the cerebrospinal system; extending especially to the lower limbs and making rather specific applications across the lumbar, the 9th dorsal and through the head and neck."

For anyone who is going through great emotional crisis or is enduring chronic strain, massage is especially recommended. In addition to obtaining a massage as often as possible, such a person can utilize the vibrator at home. One cannot do it alone, but here is how Cayce suggested using this helpful tool:

Each evening when ready to retire, apply for twenty minutes the electrically driven vibrator. Use the cup applicator down either side of the spine, as well as on the spine itself, from base of brain to the end of the spine. After applying this thoroughly to the spine, extend it across the area of the diaphragm from the back, you see—that is, crosswise the body on the lower portion of the rib area from the back. Then apply it across the sacral area, which is the lower portion of the back from the hip area, you see; and then apply it down the sciatic nerve along the thigh, and especially under the knees and to the feet themselves. Take the time, not merely as something to be gotten through with. (no. 2452–1)

The choice of oil is important for general body massage. Peanut oil and olive oil, which Cayce most frequently suggested, are the basics that we use at the Clinic. When oils are mixed at home, use half peanut oil and half olive oil. Adding rose water gives the oil a more pleasant aroma.

Why peanut oil? Cayce had this to say in one reading:

. . . yes, the lowly Peanut oil has in its combination that which will aid in creating in the superficial circulation, and in the superficial structural forces, as well as in the skin and blood, those influences that make more pliable the skin, muscles, nerves and tendons, that go to make up the assistance to structural portions of the body. Its absorption and its radiation through the body will also strengthen the activities of the structural body itself (no. 2968–1)

At the Clinic we also offer instructional massages. A husband or a wife or a friend can learn the ABCs of massage and then can regularly give a massage at home. It won't be as professional as one given by a massage therapist, but it will carry with it a lot of love and giving. Just remember that no matter what the person's condition or the treatment being given, physical therapy can be a spiritual act. Cayce said once that there is as much of God in a teaspoonful of castor oil as there is in a prayer.

We must understand, too, that each individual is like a flower. No two flowers open exactly to the same degree, even from the same rosebush. So we had better understand that the people with whom we work have a consciousness that needs to be appreciated. On one occasion, when Cayce was asked if a particular person should take castor oil by mouth, he answered, "If you have a castor oil consciousness, take castor oil." It's like the patient who comes to me and wants a shot of penicillin for his sore throat and says that every time he gets a sore throat penicillin cures it—that man has a penicillin consciousness. If I don't give him penicillin, it's not likely he'll get over the sore throat.

We try to align our therapeutic approach as much as possible with each patient's awareness and work with him or her appropriately. At the same time, we are mindful that it is not the castor oil pack, or the massage, or the prayer, or the visualization, or the herb tea that is doing the healing. For in all of these, God is manifesting and is bringing an awareness to those tissues within the body. It's as if the life force itself touches the consciousness of the cells within the human frame and they awaken and perform in their more enlightened state of awareness. That's what healing is all about.

11

Working with
the Unconscious

Every patient who comes to the Temple Beautiful Program brings along a divided consciousness. It's like a war going on between the head and the body, much as Paul said, "I do not understand my own actions. For I do not do what I want, but I do the very thing I hate" (Rom. 7:15, RSV).

We have had plenty of opportunities over many lifetimes to give input to our unconscious. It's comparable to computer programming, and it preceded our modern-day machines by thousands of years. Our programming has included many constructive thoughts, desires, and actions, so we expect them to appear when called upon. However, destructive, negative forces are there, too, put there by our bad habits. These surface also.

The problem, as I see it, is that the two are mixed together in a storage of memories within our own beings that tells our total body consciousness, "This is just how things are. This is normal, and anyone who thinks differently just does not understand where truth lies." That's not really how things are, fortunately. The real self, the soul-self, voyaging through many incarnations, has never really lost sight of that divine being which created it. The memory may have been submerged deeply by the overlay of negative, destructive impulses and actions, self-satisfying urges that become pleasures.

But fortunately we have a conscience. It is like a little child who raises its head and asks, "Why are you doing this to me?" The conscience is the voice of that soul-self which is trying to get to us, to say that we have a path to follow that has been shown to us and to ask if we are going to follow it.

However, in this seemingly never-ending battle, the wee small voice of the child is easily overpowered by our environment—our culture, even our friends and family members, our school chums. They seem to know what they are saying, and *so many* voices are heard that ask, "Why are you listening to the ramblings of that kid?"

We can clear it all up a bit by localizing the site of the war. The little kid is located in the head and neck—the gangster finds his home in the body. It is in the glands of the body—the gonads, the cells of Leydig, the adrenals, and the thymus—that our animal self reigns supreme, or *nearly* supreme.

It's indeed interesting to me that the dividing line is right at the top of the shoulders—that's where these forces line up to war with each other. And what do we find there? The thyroid gland. This is the gland that has so much to do with the will. When one is overweight, one will often say, "I just don't have the willpower to go on a *real* weight reduction program"—and mean it. The decision is never reached with some, and their excess weight leads them to serious illness from which they may never recover.

In the same way, when the gangster—who always breaks the laws for his own selfish wishes and desires, centered most often around money or power or both—demands his way inside the body consciousness, the little kid says, "I'm not sure what to do here."

Now, the strange thing is that the child has more power than the nasty gangster, who would kill and maim to get his way. But the little child so often doesn't recognize that with the power of that little gland it can choose to run the body as it wishes, and the gangster cannot prevent this. The bad guys lose the battle.

How does this crazy thing happen? Well, one other factor must be put into the context of things, since we have a problem with the little kid. It looks into the fogginess of that unconscious mind and is not really sure just when to say no, when to make its decision this way or that. The gangster is very sure of his way, since he wants only his own gain. The child may be so confused that it has forgotten its heritage and nature and just lets things ride.

The other factor is an ideal—not an idea but an ideal. If we can get that little child to listen to us enough, we can saturate that unconscious mind so thoroughly with an ideal that it will *know* what its destiny is once again and start making those decisions. Once it has a measuring stick by which to judge every action this body might be about to take, the gangster is defeated at every turn and may even change into a law-abiding citizen.

What about the ideal, then? What can we choose for our ideal? Many ideals have been set, but what can we choose as the ideal that will serve us until we are not only on the way home but actually there? I'm sure many of us could spell this out correctly, but let me quote Cayce on the choosing of an ideal, for his work is what we have been researching and trying to understand over the years since we first contacted it. The ideal is centered in the life that Jesus lived on the earth. Cayce points out that we should be asking the question, What would Jesus have me do? regarding our every question in our relationships with our fellow human beings, in our homes, and in our problems day by day. This would be an ideal sufficient to meet any of life's situations.

An ideal needs to be an ultimate goal, and in the Cayce readings and in my own concept of life as it exists, the Christ is that kind of an ideal. Cayce said, "For hath it not been given or told thee . . . 'He is the Word, He maketh all that was made, and without Him there was nothing made that was made?' And He *liveth* in the hearts and souls of those who seek to do His biddings." (no. 1326–1).

Harvey Grady spends time with every group of program participants helping them to shape their ideal. This can be done by the conscious mind, in spite of what might be coming at the present time from that little child inside, whose voice has not been heard often enough or in a manner that fits what the individual would choose as his or her ideal.

The ideal becomes then the measuring rod each person can use to guide his or her actions, so that each of the "evils" of the flesh can be eradicated in interpersonal relationships in the earth. A measuring rod allows one to measure against it a proposed action and see how it fits, how it measures, what its value is—would we see it to be maybe 75 percent or 90 percent, or maybe only 5–10 percent? That's how a measuring rod helps out. But we have to choose it first and decide to use it.

That's where the power of the will comes into play. For when we have established the ideal—the measuring rod—we *know* what to do. That is where we can run into difficulty, too, and begin to lose heart or sit in judgment on ourselves. But one of the greatest aids I've found in these readings when it comes to following up on an ideal and failing is the statement Cayce made that the try is held to Him for righteousness. That means to me that God would indeed love me even if I fail time after time. But he is interested in where I am going, not in where I am. Every try, then, that I make toward that goal is associated with the knowledge of where or what that goal is, and this is to be encouraged, not discouraged.

So a failure after setting one's ideal is not food for the judge's court but rather an effort that has been expended, even though poorly, in the right direction. Cayce also reminded us that it's better to do something wrong than to do nothing at all.

Better than doing something wrong, however, is the advice Cayce gave to a forty-five-year-old woman who had high aspirations for spiritual development. She asked how she could consciously reach the divine power that she knew was within her and be able to draw upon it to accomplish the great things she thought she was capable of. And, of course, none of these deeds was aimed at anything except the highest. Cayce reminded her that she needed to find her ideal and know what it was. He said that Jesus the Christ had promised to meet her within her own body with her own temple. And, as she meditated, she would find, "There may come,—yea, there will come,—those directions; by that constant communion with Him" (no. 2533–1). She was urged not only to meditate but to practice that consciousness in her relationships with others day by day; then would come the ability to meet all challenges with the power she knew in a prior experience.

Throughout the program, the power of choice is emphasized in working with the mind, and it is always the unconscious mind, too, that is worked with—even more since all that passes through the conscious becomes part of the unconscious.

Then the powers of the earth that have been developed and have become part of the unconscious, lying in those endocrine glands and partaking of the powers of the spiritual centers, are encouraged to arise and show themselves. They are *always* associated with other individuals, so those that are to be met this incarnation are to be found in the personalities of those we are associated with. That is the handy thing about this whole business. It's as though every other person is a mirror in which one can look and see oneself. And the mirror shows the constructive and the opposite.

The difficulties, then, that are to be worked with and clarified by choice and by the application of those qualities that are found in one's ideal are sought out and given help.

Color, Music, and Movement

One bridge that spans the gulf between the worlds of the unconscious and the conscious mind is music. Across this swinging bridge passes whatever information is needed at the moment. Music has marvelous therapeutic effects on many people.

Music and creativity have long been associated. It is often said that the universe came into being through the music of the spheres. I'm sure that the master composers tapped the higher spheres of consciousness to bring us their sublime music for our enjoyment and enlightenment. When Jesus was born, it is reported that the angels sang as a heavenly choir.

Music, then, has magic that is beyond our comprehension. Although it can be used destructively, music that lifts our spirits and touches us at the soul level becomes part of the healing process. We've seen it happen many times. Out of its healing potential have been born the schools of music therapy.

The expression that music hath charms to soothe a savage beast is profoundly true. For there is undoubtedly a savage beast in each of us. Do we kill that beast, or do we change its character? Music that soothes is one of the instruments that can accomplish that kind of healing in the human being.

We use music in a variety of unique therapies. The first one we call movement with music. It brings the participants into direct contact with music and its counterpart, color. The artistic abilities of each individual also have an opportunity to come into play and be expressed.

Erika shows participants a movie about the Kay Ortmans Wellsprings program of movement with music, then takes them out on the lawn and offers them their choice of brilliantly colored sheets that glow in the sunshine. With Mozart setting the pace, they move about—some running, some gliding, some marching as the spirit and the music move them. One finds a gladiator's blood in the veins of his memory; another one a ballerina's. They soon lose their self-consciousness at acting like children again as they move and dance around, testing their inner resources in trusting and letting go; in going deep into themselves, then feeling free once again.

The brilliant colors of the sheets bring to mind the other experiences, perhaps other times. Now and then feelings surface that have been hidden there since childhood (or even more deeply than that)— tears, joy, stresses, or dramatic events in some distant land and distant lifetime.

One person may lie down on the grass, spread-eagled, covered with the sheet, as if shot by an arrow. Another sits with orange draped around his shoulders as if in a mountain meditation cave faraway.

One woman moved slowly as if in a trance while the music flooded the yard. Later, in a sharing session, she said she was "actually in" an English mansion, looking out the windows into the yard where a friend of hers was playing. She could feel the chill of the stones and smell the mustiness of the air inside the mansion.

The music carried one of the men in the group to Rome, where he was marching in time to the drums and the trumpets, his army behind him and the captured prisoners trailing, bound and in slavery. All sorts of feelings and memories come to the surface as the music allows more traffic to cross that bridge between the conscious and the unconscious minds.

After the outdoor play with music and color and sharing, the group comes indoors, and their artistic tendencies are given full play. Using chalks and butcher paper, they draw whatever the music moves them to portray. Suddenly their unconscious appears before them in the form of symbols. A multitude of symbols may appear: pyramids, the sun, the cross, bluebirds, stars, numbers, eagles, lions and tigers, flowers, lamps, trees, lakes, and oceans. Many show up with a path or a road; it often leads to a mountain. These symbols can later be used in creating a life seal.

A life seal is a self-created or self-chosen picture of the various events, or symbols of those events, that are most meaningful to one's achieving his or her purpose in life. It can be of any shape—we encourage the artists to frame their seals and place them in their homes where they will be seen frequently. Some have circular designs, some rectangular or square. One well-known professional artist did her life seal in miniature with cardboard, but later on created it life-size in metal.

In seeking what their real purpose in life is, members of the group have a lot of assistance. Margie shows them slides of other life seals, including Edgar Cayce's, which came through a reading he gave. His shows symbols of past-life experiences that were important in fulfilling his purpose in this lifetime: the pyramid, the oasis with three palm trees, the swans, the sailboat, and the cross all within a circle. Each of us ideally can find our purpose within the framework of God's ultimate purpose for everyone. As Cayce put it, it is "to make or cause the whole of the entity's being—soul-body, soul-mind—to become more God-like, Christ-like, Christo-Christ-like, or Son-like" (no. 1483–1).

So it is that the adventure of discovery within the unlimited expanses of the mind has its start.

Visualization, Guided Imagery, Group Dynamics

Several years ago a group of doctors at Duke University published a study concerning the relationship between anger and heart disease. It showed that though a high anger-hostility index can be a personality trait, it can also be induced in people who originally do not have it. Constant criticism, harassment, and downgrading can bring it about in someone who started out "clean," in a sense.

The study also showed that whether anger and hostility is a personality trait or a problem imposed by others, it can cause heart disease and aggravate preexisting ailments. Further, it was found from reviews of death certificates and personal histories of another group of men that those whose personalities were marked by anger and hostility died of heart disease or the worsening of a preexisting physical condition sooner than statistical averages would predict.

Cayce explained what happens to us when we allow anger to possess us. He said: "Keep in that of constructive thought, because, to be sure, the thoughts of the body act upon the emotions as well as the assimilating forces. Poisons are accumulated or produced by anger or by resentment or animosity. Keep sweet!" (no. 23–3).

The way to avoid trouble is as old as the Bible. As the Old Testament proverb says, "A soft answer turneth away wrath." This means we have a choice. The target of such harassment can choose not to take on the anger-hostility trait *if* he or she is aware that this is possible *and* really wishes to avoid it. The one with the trait inborn, so to speak, can also change his or her risk for heart disease by electing to adopt a nonhostile attitude when dealing with other people. Then we must remember, too, that the hostile one and the recipient of the hostility are mirrors for each other. It reminds us of the saying, "Birds of a feather flock together."

Overcoming anger may not be easy. Professional help may be needed. Our group sessions in the program bring about many changes. Visualization experiences lead many to realize what they can do by applying their minds constructively. Visualizing oneself being kind can bring that about—it may take time, but it will happen if the process is followed consistently, persistently, and with a great deal of patience.

In the group sessions, guided imagery will often take participants down a pathway into the door of their inner temple where they meet their own higher self or their teacher. One such experience took a man down a misty path, in a robe, hearing gentle music while he moved along. He didn't know where he was going, but he knew it was right. When the mist cleared he found himself in front of a beautiful chapel. He thought it should be a cathedral, but it was too small. Inside the open door stood the figure of Jesus, who beckoned to him to enter and led him to a seat in front of a semicircle of seated persons whose faces or identity he could not make out. Then he was face to face with Jesus, and they had a deep conversation. He couldn't recall what was said, but he knew it was important, for his life was different from that point on.

How do we deal with these deep, meaningful experiences? They simply become part of one's life, like meeting an old school chum once again after many years. But the meaning behind such an experience, which no one else can see or feel or truly imagine, makes of this a new beginning in moving toward one's destiny and fulfilling one's purpose in life.

At the same time, alterations in the way one acts from that point forward mean a change for the better in health patterns. Healing, in other words, is promoted.

Some of the greatest emotional problems, which in turn have precipitated major illnesses, are guilt, fear, anger, or criticism (directed toward or away from the individual). Most if not all these emotions come from the practice of judging. Thus, in at least one of the group sessions, people find within their inner consciousness their own personal judge. And that judge keeps following them for days, until they can release the tendency to judge themselves or others. This in turn starts to release the guilt and replace the judgment with forgiveness.

Follow-up on all these opportunities, of course, comes about through individual counseling sessions, where deeper looks can be taken, and steps toward understanding oneself can be pursued.

Unfolding the Past: Be Your Own Psychic

Everyone is psychic, Edgar Cayce insisted. He defined psychic as part of the soul activity. The best evidence is that every night, when we go to sleep, we dream. We may not remember our dreams, but we *know* that everyone dreams. The dream is a psychic experience, and thus, it is an activity of the soul. It is a manifestation of one's psychic ability or soul force, Cayce said. But psychic ability has many other apsects. Cayce said that in the truest sense, psychic activity is an expression of the latent or hidden sense of the soul and spirit forces.

We give our group members' soul forces quite a workout. One whole session deals with psychometry, the art of holding an object and feeling its vibration and recognizing where it came from perhaps or what it has to tell as its own story. Some individuals who are quite psychic use psychometry to "tune in" to another person's conscious or unconscious mind. Each person in our group is given an object to feel and to tune into. They are asked what they "feel" or "think" about the object. It is rather astonishing to most of them that they can indeed know something about an object that they have never seen before.

Then, with the help of a staff member who knows what an aura looks like, they try to see one another's auras. And some of them do begin to see auras. Then they pair up and stand facing each other, looking deeply into the other's eyes, and they begin to see glimpses of past experiences that their partner has had. Are they true, or is this just imagination? Imagination, you know, is only the creative ability of the individual working its way through the autonomic/unconscious mind of the body. So maybe it is imagination.

Cayce wanted to use whatever soul or psychic forces he had gained primarily for the welfare of others, but he said that these same powers are latent in each and every individual. He indicated that the psychic ability within each person "may be developed by application, not just by thinking—but by applying. To think is to act, to some; to others it is only an interesting pastime. *Application* is a different condition" (no. 256–2).

We can touch in on this soul power, but we need always to be aware of its source, and that the one Source's desires are to do good. Ignoring this and using psychic power for selfish purposes creates penalties for the user. In the Bible, it's called reaping what you have sown. Or you might look at it this way—you have defied God's will, so you will have the opportunity to experience someone you love defying your will. Because you have been defiant in exercising your

will, someone will be quite defiant to you. In the process, one moves
farther away from one's purpose in life.

Thus, the very life force we use moment by moment is truly soul
power—not just the unusual abilities like remembering past lives,
having magnificent dreams, or giving readings from a deep, extended
state of consciousness.

All things can be learned, but for what purpose—do they fit into
that purpose for which you came into this incarnation? If not, it's
better to use the energies that are at your disposal to create those
events and actions that *do* move you in a purposeful direction. These
are the reminders we give each of the group, but we encourage them
to test themselves—perhaps some of these capabilities have been
worked on in past lives and can be used purposefully this time.

In the afternoon, we let them try a recall experience. We call it
music, movement, and memory. They search out a place of memory,
somewhere in the house, where they can lie down with a light cover
and a pillow, making sure that their notebook is by their side, so they
can write down what comes to them. Then, with a short period of
relaxation, reading them something about their psychic abilities and
the purposes therein, we remind them that they should not rely upon
others but look within and find that still, small voice that can bring
them what they need at the moment. For they are indeed manifestations of God's love and are one with him.

We remind them that during the period of the music, there will
come flashes at times of material experiences in the earth—sojourns—and that in the process of becoming quiet with the music
and becoming receptive, as one would in meditation, one will gain
much—not so much as what is ordinarily termed psychic but rather
an awakening of the true self and a part of one's self that has been
lost or gained in past experiences. Bringing these to the awareness in
the present time—especially where love is a part of one's action—can
become a blessing in one's life.

Then, a short meditation is followed by a guided imagery where
they are led up the steps of their Temple of Wisdom to meet their
teacher and then on in to find the records they seek. They are next

gently instructed to move quietly, without talking to each other, from the room where they have started the process to their place of memory.

The music takes over at that point, and an hour and a half later they are brought back to the central gathering place to share their experiences. Nearly everyone at first tries to explain their memories as just imagination. They think they probably saw this place sometime when they were visiting another land, which may indeed be so. But the imagination is a creative portion of one's mind and can bring more than just immediate life flashbacks to awareness.

Three people in one group shared memories of being in a ballroom in France, a magnificent place where they were dancing. One remembered recognizing one or two others. Another said that a man burst into the ballroom with the information that the French Revolution had started.

All had written down what came to them as they allowed the music to stir up the passage of memories from unconscious to conscious. And these were all given a tentative validity. We recognize that some may be total fabrications, but there are flashes of insight that should not be dismissed, and sometimes whole portions of a past life.

So, what good will these be? Cayce said that we look to the past for understanding, and we look to the future with hope. The understanding brings us just a bit closer to that goal, that oneness that has been promised from the beginning. And the bringing to light of a past experience frequently gives us great insight about why we have tendencies that seem to touch off difficulties in this life. Then we can work toward cleansing them from our minds—reprogramming the body as one would do with a computer if it were printing out the wrong information.

The negative or destructive tendency always has its counterpart in one that is constructive. Isn't it the inborn desire of every human being to be helpful? One sees it in the meanest of characters, such as the domineering male supervisor who shows such gentleness in his touch when his little girl meets him on the sidewalk as he returns home from work. His gentle side is there; it needs to be amplified first through recognition, then cemented through application—even though it may be difficult—in relationship with his family, his friends, his co-workers, even those he doesn't like.

These seem to be the benefits obtained from sessions in which those in physical and mental difficulties search out what past-life experiences have to give in the way of advice and help.

Unlocking the Dreams

Some years ago, I had a dream that sounded foolish to me at first but that all of us—our study group people—worked at. It began with my awareness that an Egyptian ruler had placed another man in charge of running that country. It seemed as though I was that man—much like Joseph and his job in the biblical story (Gen. 39:4). In running the country, I had an assistant to whom I had given the responsibility of putting away the treasures of the country in a safe place. He was absolutely trustworthy and would always speak the truth; thus I would have the secrets of the country always available through him.

The interesting part of the dream was that he was called the Fool because he would never say anything except no. That was his whole vocabulary. Everyone else thought he was a fool and so would pay no attention to him. I knew, however, that he was wise, that he knew where all the treasures of the country were put away, and that he was totally honest. I could always get information from him simply by posing questions that would get a yes or no answer.

Our interpretation of the dream was that the Fool was actually my dream self, my dream capability. It was showing me that if I wanted an answer, I merely needed to make a decision that something was so before I went to sleep, and then ask my "Fool" if that was right. No answer meant yes. If I did get an answer, it would always be a resounding no.

Later on, I found that I really needed to make choices and go in a particular direction, in a sense, and only then ask for guidance. My dreams would contain a positive or negative kind of feeling or action in them, and that would be my answer. Gladys and I have since used the dreams for guidance.

Everyone's dreams will develop in their own specific way if we pay attention. It's like a schoolteacher who gives more care and guidance to those who are asking, usually by the attitude they show toward the subject being taught.

From the first day onward, our participants who are trying to develop their own Temple Beautiful (whether they know it or not) are given instructions about their dream life, and each morning during the breakfast hour, we discuss dreams. One or two of the program people have earned the title "Resident Dreamer" because each morning they had a dream to report.

I always suggest purchasing a spiral notebook for recording dreams, printing in large letters on the front, MY DREAM BOOK. Then one can start numbering dreams, dating them, identifying where one had the dream, and leaving space for listing the symbols and interpretations at the end of each dream. I also suggest that one write down the problem/question that was being considered by the dreamer before going to sleep, for often this is what the dream is all about.

The dream works with the unconscious mind, which remains active during sleep. All the bodily functions continue, monitored by that same autonomic nervous system and its glandular attachments, the computer-like part of ourselves where all the past-life memories are stored and from which guidance can come—for it is there that the higher self or the Christ within dwells.

From the soul-self can come aid in keeping the conscious being on the path toward where we really want to go. And it does come, but in many forms. It often has very practical advice for the physical body. This is again natural and to be expected, for the body, mind, and spirit are really one, and aid for the body is like aid for the mind.

One of Gladys's patients told her about a dream that she thought was talking about her diet. She had been told by Gladys to increase her intake of vitamin C. She had done so, then had this dream: "I was walking along the sidewalk, returning home from the grocery store with a bag of carrots in my arms. Suddenly a rotten lemon fell off the tree overhead and into the bag of carrots." The two of them decided the dream meant that she was getting too much vitamin C and should cut down on it and, instead, get more vitamin A. It could have meant also that the vitamin C she was taking was really threatening to harm her supply of vitamin A.

Sometimes we dream for others. At one point when my life involved a great deal of turmoil because our Clinic was undergoing significant stress, I was reacting with a lot of resistance and anger. My friend James McCready had this dream:

> I was standing beside a rough cinder path that came from my right and led down to the left into darkness. Striding down the path past me from the right was a great, beautiful Bengal tiger. Behind him, hanging on to his tail with both hands and with bloody feet spread as if to stop the progress of the tiger, was you, Bill McGarey, hanging on for dear life. As you got opposite where I was standing, you said, "What in heck will I do, James?" I said, "Well, you dern fool, LET GO!" You got so mad that you let go of the tiger's tail and knocked me down.

That was the end of the dream. Needless to say, I let go of the adrenal-like activities in my life where stress had put me on edge. (The adrenal gland produces the fight–flight response in the body.) We need to learn from every dream if we possibly can and then put what we've learned into action.

When one considers the inhumane manner in which many people are treated today, the atrocities, the selfishness and greed that still abound in this world, then it is no wonder that humanity must in some way account for these wrongs. There is a law—"Whatsoever a man soweth, that shall he also reap" (Gal. 6:7)—that says that everything that has been meted must be met. Some call it karma. To me, all this means that we cannot do something physically or mentally in this dimension of life without having it confront us later on in some manner.

The beauty of the fact that the mind is the builder, however, is that we don't really need to face exactly the same thing. If we have done something hurtful to another, for instance, we can meet it in the way that exercises a higher law than the one we call karma, the law of cause and effect. The higher law is that when we meet that condition again, we can wipe it off the books by exercising the qualities of understanding, forgiveness, and patience.

These qualities are aspects of love, and I suspect that God is love and that all God wants us to do is to allow ourselves to be purveyors of love in the same way he has been. This is accomplished through a higher consciousness that replaces the one that calls for anger, for vengeance, for getting even. And then, as in the dream, we can take the guidance and let go of the tiger's tail.

This is what happened to Susie, one of our Temple Beautiful patients who was a divorced mother of two children. Her former husband had been imprisoned for child molestation. After his release he disappeared, taking the children with him. Sick with grief and worry, Susie started having nightmares. Night after night it was nearly always the same: she would approach her former husband's house, see him inside with the two children, make her way into the house grasping a long, sharp knife she had hidden from sight. In her dream she would confront him, then attempt to stab him in the heart. Quick as a flash, he would snatch one of the children and hold the child in front of his chest; the knife would go into the child's heart, killing it and leaving blood all over Susie's hands. She would awaken in tears. This repeated nightmare continued as she entered the program, two years after his disappearance. The failure of detectives to find her children increased her anguish.

When she revealed it to the group, she was told, "You need to let go of the anger and the hate. You need to forgive. You need to ask higher powers to care for the children. You need to remember that each person chooses where and for what purpose he or she is born. You can be free of the heartbreak. The children will suffer less if you let go."

Susie could not accept this interpretaion immediately. But as the program went on she resisted less and less. Then, just before the session ended, she had an entirely different dream. She was again outside her former husband's house. She looked inside and saw her children playing, happy and contented. She had no knife in her hand. She smiled, rolled out her sleeping bag on the lawn outside the house, and lay down, looking up at the stars. That was the end of the dream— and when she finished telling it, everyone in the room applauded.

Susie had applied a higher law. Not only was she relieved of a stress that eventually would have caused her serious physical illness, but her act of forgiveness had to have had a beneficial effect on the development of her children, for the dream was not giving her any information but the truth.

As we unlock our dreams, then, we begin searching out the events of the past, start to process our understanding of what has been going on, and then learn what to do to create a solution that is totally constructive and helpful to those involved.

You see, Susie somewhere in a past life had manufactured the pattern of living that was to serve as a mirror so that she could see herself now in a different light. Then she touched on the secret that stays hidden from so many, that could and did bring healing of the mind, the emotions, and certainly the soul. And she acted preventively to keep from becoming ill.

In Cayce's words, Susie's dilemma was solved because she followed this advice:

> *Love*, then, *Divine*; as was manifested in Jesus of Nazareth, must be the rule—yea, the measuring stick—the rod, by which ye shall judge thy motives, thy impulses, thy associations. For without Him there is not anything made that is made—to endure.
>
> *Man* may produce the stumbling-stones, God alone—in the heart of man—may make them stepping-stones!
>
> Love the Lord, keep His ways, manifest them in the every walk of life. Let others do as they may, but as for thee and thy house, *love*, obey the *living* God! (no. 1497–1)

12

Energies at Work
to Heal the Body

To AWAKEN IN THE morning and find that the right side of your face is paralyzed is a very traumatic experience. Most of us have felt a portion of the face go numb with anesthesia before dental work. That's uncomfortable enough—our speech comes out distorted; our face feels "funny"; and we become very uneasy in the presence of others. But when the entire right side of your face is suddenly completely paralyzed, that *is* traumatic.

When this happened to Darlene, a housewife who had never been a patient at the Clinic before, she thought at first she had had a stroke. But the paralysis didn't appear to affect any other part of her body. She had just returned from an auto trip four days before, and she had slept with the ceiling fan going the night before. We diagnosed her conditions as Bell's palsy, meaning that a large peripheral nerve to the face is not working, causing that side of the face to be flaccid.

The outlook for one who has Bell's palsy is not totally bright. Sometimes it persists and never allows the body to return fully to normal. Most of the time, in my experience, it will last a number of weeks unless something really constructive is done for it. My father-in-law suffered such a paralysis the day after he had driven several hundred miles with the car window open on the driver's side and the air blowing on his face. That was back in the fifties, when we had no electrotherapy available or even knew about it. It was eight weeks before his face regained its normal function.

Darlene, on the other hand, benefited by new therapies in the field of energy medicine. The day after her diagnosis, in our Energy Medicine Department she was given an hour's treatment with our acuscope and myopulse instruments. This equipment is designed to identify and show on the monitor screen those electrical energies near the surface of the body that are abnormal. Those problem areas can be treated until the energy flow is more normal. The usual name given such therapy is transcutaneous electrical neurostimulator (TENS) treatments. The effectiveness of such treatments lies in restoring the nerve supply to a given area back to normal.

After the first treatment, Darlene reported much improvement. Her face felt better, and it was beginning to move. After her second treatment six days later, the paralysis was mostly gone, and she was just about where she had started before that ceiling fan caused the facial paralysis—just a bit of tearing of the eye, but the eye would close normally and the rest of the findings were normal. I was excited, but she even more so, and that is the pleasure in practicing medicine, seeing the body restored to normal. After a third treatment a week later no problems remained.

A three-week checkup proved that all was well. Darlene had had a severe problem that turned out to be a very pleasing life experience. The woman who worked with her in applying the therapy also benefited, for she not only loves to work with the equipment but also knows the value of being in a psychological mode of giving and healing in order to help the patient gain the most from the therapy.

Justin had a different kind of experience, but just as thrilling. Normally a very physical twenty-year-old who was active in sports, Justin developed general weakness and malaise. His symptoms pointed to what is called Epstein-Barr virus syndrome, caused by a virus that seems to be related to the one associated with mononucleosis. This condition is most often seen following an episode of infectious mononucleosis, which Justin had had.

He had seen a specialist for the problem, and unfortunately when a biopsy was taken of a lymph node in the right shoulder area a nerve was cut. The result was a progressive atrophy of the entire upper shoulder group of muscles.

Two months after the biopsy, when he came to the Clinic for the first time, he could not move his right arm properly, and all his hopes for participating in sports of any kind seemed to be gradually disappearing. Justin was pretty despondent. We sent him to our Energy Medicine Department for acuscope treatment. After six weeks of therapy with the acuscope, his neurologist examined him again and reported that his nerve had begun to heal and that the muscles were regenerating.

The therapy continued weekly, and just eleven weeks after his first visit, Justin showed full range of motion in the right arm, full regrowth of the muscle girdle, and, for all intents and purposes, full return of normal activity. Justin, of course, was elated about his recovery. With his shoulder back to normal, Justin still had to go through a period of time working to overcome the Epstein-Barr virus problem. All problems of the human body are not reasonably corrected at one time. That is probably good as far as the consciousness of the individual is concerned, for each experience is an opportunity for soul growth—and Justin took advantage of that experience. He has another coming.

Longevity

If a nerve can be regenerated and bring new life to a group of muscles with the administration of electrical impulses brought from the outside to the surface of the skin, it stands to reason that the same power from inside the skin of a salamander is being replicated by a mechanism outside the body. Whatever the mechanism, whether derived from that Source of life within the human frame or not, it is called regeneration, and these powers that can bring that about inside certainly lead to health and long life.

Longevity, and the rejuvenation procedures that lead to it, hold a rather prominent place in the Edgar Cayce readings. Likewise, in the thoughts of all of us, longevity commands a degree of respect. If we don't live a long time, we think, just what is the alternative? And there are few who choose that.

The road to long life is often difficult to discern and, like most things, is discovered sometimes by those who were not actively looking for it. Charlie Smith is an example.

Born in Liberia in Africa in 1842, he was captured as a teenager, brought to this country before the Civil War, and sold into slavery (part of our country's unhappy heritage and subsequent karma). He lived not only to gain his freedom but to enjoy over one hundred years of life as a free American. He finally moved on to another dimension in 1979, at age 137, leaving his throne as the oldest man in the United States. His seventy-three-year-old son attended his funeral.

To live longer than a hundred years is really not that unusual. In Hebron, Israel, Jajj Yousef Awad Mohammed Burkan died in 1980 at the age of 150. He had helped dig the Suez Canal in the 1860s, had been a soldier in the Turkish Army for thirty-five years, and had farmed the land near Hebron for the last seventy years of his life. He had married three times, the last occasion when he was one hundred years old. Burkan must have been like Moses is reported to have been at the age of one hundred twenty—eyes clear, natural forces unabated. What makes long life such as this possible? Cayce said we have the power to remain youthful and active:

> For, the ability of each functioning of the body-forces is to reproduce itself, and as long as this continues the body keeps not only young but active—mentally, spiritually, physically—unless it be drugged by its own ego. (no. 3042–1)

Burkan's story tells us that the life force really controls the body, not the reverse. Getting old does not make one die.

Rejuvenation, Regeneration

All of us have the power to rebuild and rejuvenate the body. If we keep this in mind as a true possibility, our apprehension of disease and disability can be dissipated, and the wonders of the human body can be appreciated, explored, and utilized in the interest of enjoying good health.

To rejuvenate is to renew one's youth. To regenerate is much the same—to restore the body or portions of it to their original condition. In regenerating a limb, either human or animal, Becker's work showed that a blastema (a mass capable of growth and differentiation) formed—a reworking, in a sense, of the process of embryological development—returning to the first stages of cellular growth, so that the limb that is already there in its finer energy form can be filled out, perhaps even as it was done in utero. It is the dedifferentiation of cells back to primordial forms and then their redifferentiation to form those physical manifestations of the finer energy body.

Cayce's description takes this process from the spiritual side of our being and cuts across many disciplines of thinking. Here is what he told a woman who had a rather severe spinal curvature:

> It is self-evident that it will not be possible in the beginning to release those nerves that are pinched, where curvatures exist in the spine. But these may be gradually changed. For each cycle, every element, every condition must renew itself; else there becomes or is set up greater deterioration than creation. And each element, each organ, each functioning of the body throughout, is capable of reproducing itself. How?
>
> Not merely from the ability of the glands to take from that assimilated those elements needed, but in each atom, in each corpuscle, is Life. Life is that ye worship as God.
>
> If God be with you, and you *choose* to use those elements in His creation that cause each atom, each corpuscle, to become more and more aware of that creative influence, there may then be brought resuscitation. May there not be created, then, health rather than disease, disorder, confusion? (no. 2968–1)

Cayce talked about regeneration on many occasions. He said that the body basically is an atomic structure—a storehouse of influences and forces from outside, like emotional reactions and food. The body continually rebuilds itself from within, and it has that ability to rejuvenate or to regenerate. There's a catch, however. The rebuilding is according to the mental attitude that one holds toward ideals and how one applies those ideals in relationship to others and also to one's self. So we could think of the body rebuilding and regenerating itself as long as the body's atoms conform to a spiritual ideal and action takes place in line with that ideal.

How can we tell when regeneration is coming about in our bodies? This difficulty is probably one of the largest stumbling blocks preventing our accepting the concept or having the faith that it is true and acting on it. And yet we have seen evidence of regeneration in many ways. For instance, have you ever cut your hand or your finger, and then had the laceration stitched? It healed up in several days, then you had the stitches removed. It left a scar—and a scarring is not regeneration. It is simply closing up the skin so the body is relatively whole again, and it uses what we call scar tissue, not normal epithelium.

If, on the other hand, this laceration happened twenty years ago, and you can no longer find any evidence of where the hand was injured, that is regeneration, for the body has replaced the scar tissue with what was there originally. Scarring happens consistently, also, if sutures are not used to close the wound. But regeneration comes about sooner than if there is need to close the wound surgically. Massaging the scar with castor oil will hasten the regeneration.

The body renews itself entirely—every atom—over the course of seven years. That means that the atoms of the body restructure themselves around and in vibratory accord with the real energy body (that we've had from the beginning) and eliminate the scar through a gradual process of regeneration. Some scars and most birthmarks fail to be regenerated. This is due to failure to follow the laws that are involved, which Cayce explained rather clearly.

Thousands of my patients over the years have had their tonsils removed, yet I often find that the tonsil tissue has grown back. The cells that were removed surgically have grown back to fill out that pattern that is found in the real energy body.

I'm sure some doctors have been sued by women who became pregnant after the fallopian tubes have been tied off surgically to prevent pregnancy. It is well known that following surgery, one or both of those tubes may regenerate and become open again so that the ovum from the ovary can course down to the sperm, thus supporting pregnancy once again.

Fingertips have regrown in children and adults after accidents destroyed the tissue, necessitating the amputation. Regeneration is really no longer a thing we wonder about; rather we ask, "When can it happen to me?" I think Cayce's readings give valuable insight on that, as far as it concerns overcoming the illnesses that afflict us.

Electrotherapy

We frequently see people like Darlene, with Bell's palsy, and Justin, with muscular atrophy, overcoming considerable difficulties of the body. At the clinical level, their recovery gives us a glimpse of the future potential of using electricity on the functioning organism. And it gives us promise of wider application of energy medicine in the healing arts.

Creating a greater balance in the electrical activities of the body improves the functioning of the organs themselves, improves the co-ordination of the various organs, and brings relief to those that have been under strain. It is important that health and relief of stress and strain come about first in the cells, then in the organs themselves, then in the balance that must be struck among all the life-support activities. For it is these functional systems that allow the structural forces—the bones, muscles, and ligaments—of the body to work adequately.

Electrotherapy, as used by our Energy Medicine Department, takes many forms. The TENS devices mentioned earlier bring about changes within the body through their electrical input across the barrier of the skin. Acupuncture has worked to change the electricity in the body through needles penetrating the skin. Inside and beneath the skin, the cells that are stimulated have the ability to create electricity that then moves along the meridians that were described by the Chinese literally thousands of years ago. The electricity acting within the body then does its work. At the Clinic, we use an electromagnetic field unit (ETA) that moves the patient through the earth's electromagnetic field and brings about a change in the electric flow within the body through one of the laws of physics, which dictates that any change in a conductor of electricity or in the field around that conductor occurs simultaneously in both. Thus, when the two fields change because of the movement of the table, with the patient lying on it, there occurs a change in the electrical flow through the patient's body. Other electrotherapy devices are being studied as part of our research program.

When one lies on the ETA, the unit is turned on, and the bed slowly rotates laterally, moving the patient up and down in a circular path from one side to the other. The electrical field that always surrounds the human body then is moved through not only the earth's field but an electrical current between the head and the foot of the bed. The effect is very relaxing; it often serves the patient by reducing stress while at the same time inducing a slightly altered state of consciousness. Visualization is often enhanced, and some people experience clearer episodes of guided imagery. We recognize the value of the ETA as a psychiatric couch. Counseling becomes a part of the therapy during its use and is much more effective then, since the unconscious mind is more readily available, with its memories of past lives and difficulties in this life.

Unusual things happen sometimes during this therapy. Pain is often totally relieved, sometimes permanently. A friend and patient who had been suffering from angina pectoris for some time was trying to use natural methods of restoring health rather than taking medicine. One day while on the ETA, he was relaxed and feeling very comfortable when he suddenly heard a "pop" inside his chest. That was nearly ten years go, and he's never had any problem with angina since. None of us were able to venture an educated guess just what the "pop" really was.

Harvey Grady's study of one group of twelve patients in the Temple Beautiful Program (*Electro-Therapy Concepts from the Edgar Cayce Readings*, A.R.E Clinic, Phoenix, 1982) offered evidence that the ETA had a significant effect, when used with sensitive attendants, in helping patients gain greater insight into their own being. Summarized, its findings were as follows:

1. Reduction of stress occurred 100 percent of the time.
2. Relief (decrease or loss) of pain occurred 100 percent of the time, when pain was evident at the start of a session.
3. Attitudes and emotions became more positive 86 percent of the time.
4. Patients experienced expansion of consciousness 80 percent of the time, gaining valuable insights.
5. Patients made significant decisions about the direction of their personal lives 35 percent of the time during therapy sessions.

Though not all patients experience the last three benefits, when individuals are already determined to alter their lives for the better, they become open to life changes, and more come about as they progress.

Biofeedback does not treat the body but teaches the mind to control one of the body functions. Temperature control of the finger, for instance, can be monitored by attaching a thermistor to one of the fingers. Then, as one concentrates, or relaxes, or moves the body, or relaxes the shoulders, or makes the mind calm one can see the temperature of that finger going up or down. One continues working with the body until able to produce the desired effect.

The thermistor registers the temperature of the finger; that is, gives feedback on what the subject's body is doing, and that is why the procedure is called biofeedback. A number of body measurements can be monitored and feedback given in the form of sounds or readings on an instrument, and thus one can learn what to do *oneself* to cause the body to perform this or that function. It may be by simply closing the eyes that one relaxes better; the biofeedback instrument would then give that information back, verifying that one's doing a good job. It may be necessary to relax the shoulders or assume a different position in the chair, even lie down. One may need to visualize the body relaxing. Part of biofeedback is learning suggestions to give to the body like, "My shoulders are warm, relaxed, and comfortable." This instruction may need to be repeated two or three times, then followed with directions to other parts of the body. All the time, feedback from the body is being received about how well one is doing.

Heartbeat rate can be controlled in this manner; high blood pressure can be lowered; skin potential can be altered—even the activity of the lymphocytes in the bloodstream can be controlled by these methods learned through biofeedback training. Exercises developed through this method of training are called autogenic exercise, an important activity for those who are going through the Temple Beautiful Program.

Whatever therapy is used, however, the following reading gives insight into the approach we take and the concepts underlying that approach, along with the promises that come from it. Cayce said that the electricity that is given therapeutically to the body is a manifestation of creative forces or God. If we recognize this truth, if we see that Creative Force active from nature in our bodies and feel it and know that it is so, then we rebuild or revivify our bodies and "by the creating in every atom of its being the knowledge of the activity of this Creative Force or Principle as related to spirit, mind, body—all three are renewed" (no. 1299–1).

13

Healing with
the Palma Christi

Of all the many therapies I have used in my practice, none can compare with castor oil in its healing qualities and its variety of therapeutic applications. Sometimes it seems as though castor oil is good for everything that ails us. At the Clinic we use it externally and internally, often experimentally, and we almost never fail to get good results.

The amazing thing is that no one really understands why castor oil is so effective. We are conducting research to try to determine the key to its healing powers. More amazing is that most modern doctors don't use it, either because they don't believe it works as well as I know that it does or because they think of it as an old-fashioned home remedy that has been superseded by modern medicine. If all medicines were as effective, we would have hardly any sick people. I have used it successfully on patients suffering from everything from appendicitis to tumors, from hyperactivity to slipped discs. One of my patients told me it was the best tranquilizer she had ever used. Gladys and I even use it on our pets.

I began using castor oil packs on the 1960s because they were recommended in the Cayce readings. The pack we use is simply a piece of clean white wool (cotton will do if wool is not available) flannel soaked in castor oil, applied to the abdomen or the ankle or finger or whatever part is ailing. (See Appendix for full instructions on using a pack.) Cayce suggested it for many ailments.

Castor oil is derived from the bean of the *Ricinus communis* plant, which grows in many parts of the world—India, Africa, Brazil, and in the Arizona desert near my home. The seeds are extremely poisonous if eaten, but its beans are valued commercially, mostly because the oil has many industrial applications. It is used for making paints used by artists and dyes for textiles, for processing foods, and for lubricating jet airplanes. It is a great irony that our machine age has demonstrated how versatile castor oil is by inventing many industrial applications for it while overlooking its many applications for the most wonderful machine of all, the human body.

Cayce was not the discoverer of its value. Castor oil has been used for centuries. A patient for whom I used a castor oil pack on the abdomen told me she had seen the same therapy used by her grandmother in Yugoslavia, where it was used for colic and many other conditions. It was evidently known in the Middle Ages, when some perceptive person called the castor bean plant the Palma Christi—the Palm of Christ—perhaps because its gloriously green leaves take the shape of a hand. Whether its therapeutic value was known then, we can only guess, but it probably was, at least to some extent. An ancient document, the Ebers Papyrus (ca. 1550 B.C.), mentions using castor oil eyedrops to protect the eyes against irritation.

In this country and others it has been used as a laxative for scores of years. An American physician early in this century wrote about his determined Scottish aunt who regarded a "crumb o' oil," as she used to call it, "as a universal remedy of exceeding potency in both moral and physical contingencies; and indeed, there is no doubt of its efficiency as a cleaner." (See Montgomery, D. W., in Bibliography.)

Cayce, however, perceived its versatility. He recommended that it be taken internally on only a few occasions, but he often suggested external applications, undoubtedly because he had insight into the mystery of why the Palma Christi is so effective. Why does the castor bean produce such a miraculous oil? What happens internally to facilitate healing when we apply that oil to the skin? When we discover the answers to these questions, we will know a lot more about the magic of healing than science has thus far discovered.

In the more than twenty-five years that we have been using castor oil packs on our patients, we have applied them on virtually every part of the human body. To give you an idea of our experience, let me just quote from the experiences some of our patients have reported. The results are surprising, to say the least, amazing to some individuals, and unbelievable to others:

Swelling of the Fingers. Swelling of the left middle finger between the interphalangeal joints bothered Edna Atkins, but she put up with the swelling for many weeks before actually treating the finger. She had heard how good castor oil is for many things but had not tried it.

> I finally got out some oil one evening while watching television and just rubbed around the second joint awhile. I did this two evenings, leaving it on when I went to bed.
>
> The third night I was again going to rub the joint, but could not find the spot any longer. I couldn't even be sure which hand or finger it was, as there was no sign of swelling or difference between any fingers any longer!

She didn't know the diagnosis, but the cure was great!

A Growth on the Eyelid. Regarding the eyes, an A.R.E member told me his experience: He had developed a growth in the corner of one eye, with surgery apparently just around the corner. He deferred temporarily while he

> gently massaged it every night for five minutes with castor oil. After about three or four months, it did not get bigger . . . but did not disappear. In the back of my mind, I remembered a Cayce reading that suggested some bicarbonate of soda with the castor oil. Thought it worth a try. After the massage, I put a tiny dab of bicarbonate of soda on the growth. The growth got very irritated and sore for a few days . . . fell off, and never returned again. Did not even leave a scar.

Pregnancy. We've used packs to maintain the pregnancy when miscarriage threatened—and were successful. We've had patients wear packs throughout most of their pregnancy because they felt they needed it. One of our patients many years ago had two miscarriages, never being able to carry pregnancy to full term. She started to bleed at about the third month again and called Gladys on the phone. Gladys told her to get in bed and elevate the foot of the bed and put a castor oil pack on without the heating pad and keep it there. She stayed in bed two weeks. But she continued using the pack at least two or three times every week until she delivered a normal lovely little baby girl. We call it the castor oil baby.

Some time ago we received a letter from a woman who teaches mothers how to have a normal pregnancy. She wanted to share her experiences during her own home birthing.

> I began using castor oil on my skin when I was pregnant with my third child. I rubbed castor oil into my abdomen and let the oil soak into my skin. It's interesting to me, being a pregnancy and childbirth educator for the past ten years, that although my daughter was five weeks postmature, the placenta and she were both in optimal condition at birth. . . . One of the other benefits of castor oil was the absence of new stretch marks. My daughter was eight and a half pounds and twenty-one inches at birth. Labor and delivery were medically "uneventful."

She had some difficulties with the baby afterward, with baby's skin becoming infected, but liberal portions of castor oil brought that to a halt, and the skin was normal within a week.

Joint Pain. A middle-aged Arkansas man wrote that he had suffered from pain in his ankles since he was a teenager. He rubbed castor oil into each joint for four nights; the pain went away, and had not returned by the time he sent his letter, three months later. He has also used castor oil for other painful spots on his legs, clearing them up overnight without reoccurrence.

Some years ago, I treated a woman for a sprained ankle in the emergency room of a local hospital. X-rays showed she had no fracture, but her ankle was quite swollen and giving her considerable pain. I applied an elastic bandage to her ankle and instructed her in how to put on a castor oil pack at home. She'd never heard of that. Two days later, she came to the office and told me that when she left the hospital she thought, "This is crazy—what can castor oil do? But, since I don't have anything else to treat the ankle with, I'll use the castor oil." And she did. She reported that within forty-eight hours, neary all the swelling was gone, and the pain left her after six hours.

Skin Keratosis. One of our patients had a dry, thickened area on his forearm and wanted to know if he should see a skin specialist. The attending doctor said, "I told him I felt it was benign but gave him a dermatologist's address. Before he left the office, I applied a bandage with drops of castor oil on it to the lesion and told him to apply one twice a day. It ended up that he did not go to the specialist, and the lesion sloughed off in just a couple of weeks."

Lymph Node Enlargement. A woman of eighty-two who had been thriving under the various therapies for rebuilding the body that Edgar Cayce suggested, came in to see me about a lump that had developed in the right side of her neck near the angle of her jaw, very close to the base of the ear. There was no evidence of any difficulty that would cause a lymph node in that area to be enlarged; X-rays of the chest were done, laboratory tests were performed, and still no causation was uncovered.

Surgery was postponed. The tumor was the size of a hazelnut and quite firm. My patient began applying castor oil packs to that area, not wanting to have surgery. In two weeks' time it had been reduced to the size of a small pea, and one month later the lump was completely gone.

It was probably a lymph node, perhaps draining a distant skin irritation that we did not discover. No other information was uncovered, however, and the patient remained in excellent shape—another story about how castor oil can work even when one does not know or really understand everything that is going on.

Insomnia. A dear friend of ours once hated to travel because any sort of activity would keep her awake. Even under normal conditions, it was difficult for her to sleep normally. Finally, she took a pledget of cotton, soaked it with castor oil, and used it as an earplug on each side. It produced the best sleep she had experienced in years, and now she uses it regularly and with continued success in overcoming insomnia.

Ear Infection. In many cases this same kind of earplug is effective in the treatment of ear infections. One of my correspondents uses this idea differently. She fashions the plug and inserts it *after* she has instilled castor oil into the ear canal. She reports "quick relief from pain" and apparent resolution of the infection. She also uses liberal applications of the oil to take care of acne, cuts and scratches, and small infections of the skin. Her children have come to know the oil of the Palma Christi well.

Fussy Ten-month-old Child. A child can be fussy in many ways, but Nicky woke up every night just about every hour on the hour and cried as though in pain. The child's grandmother advised applying a castor oil pack to his tummy every night while he was eating his dinner. She later received this report from her son:

Saturday night	before using packs: up 3½ hours.
Sunday night	first night after using pack: up 2½ hours.
Monday night	second night: up for a couple of minutes at midnight and again briefly at 5 A.M.
Tuesday night	third night: up at midnight for half an hour. Up at 4:00 A.M. for a couple of minutes.
Wednesday night	up at 11:00 A.M. for half hour. Up at 2:30 A.M. briefly.
Thursday night	up *lots* of times.
Friday night	sixth night: was an angel for the first time while we rode a long way to shopping center, and was good while we were there. Woke for a couple of minutes once in the night.

| Saturday night | seventh night: woke at 5:00 A.M., drank juice, and went back to sleep until 8:30. |
| Sunday and last night | a nice boy all day, woke only for a couple of minutes at 4:00 and at 5:30. Slept until a little after 6:00. |

Hyperactive Child. One of our patients literally tore up magazines in the examining room while his mother told Gladys that she just couldn't handle him. He was about four and a half years old and was all over the room, opening drawers and not sitting still for a moment. Because he had a bit of a bowel problem too, Gladys told the mother to put a castor oil pack on his tummy while he was watching television. The next week when he came in he was a different child. It was our first experience using these packs for hyperactivity. The boy continued to use the packs regularly three or four times a week and became a normal five-year-old youngster.

Hay Fever. From a friend from India, we learned of an allergy therapy that he had been using for years with his patients. It consisted simply of using a dropperful of castor oil on the tongue at night—no packs needed. Another man wrote me that he had much trouble for many years with what he called "grass fever." Antihistamines offered little relief, and most of his comfort came from an air purifier. He started using castor oil drops, taking them in the morning instead of at bedtime, in a teaspoonful of ginger ale.

The result was extremely gratifying. "I had no 'grass fever' symptoms until about the middle of June, when for a period of two weeks I had some mild effects which were hardly noticeable. I found that I could sleep with the bedroom windows open during the early period and later period of the usual sensitivity duration, which I couldn't possibly have done before."

As a side benefit, he found that his voice was clear and he was able to perform his duties much better as a tourist guide at one of the historical houses in his area. Cayce, in one of his readings, said that allergies were for the most part a fad. I have not figured that one out yet.

Mosaic Wart. One of my patients told me the following story about her daughter living in Boston who developed a wart on her heel that had markings like those one sees on a map.

> When treatment with medications and shaving the affected area proved of no avail after two years the doctor recommended surgery to remove the offending part of her heel. The day before the operation I talked with her on the telephone and convinced her to cancel the cutting, and the next day, since I live in Virginia Beach, I went to the A.R.E. Library to see what they said about warts. Of course, I found castor oil as a specific so I called my daughter and told her to soak the heel of a wool sock in castor oil and wear it with a pair of old tennis shoes that were expendable. She started to follow those instructions on July 10, 1984; by August 10, one month later, the mosaic wart was gone and has never returned again. Today her heel is perfectly normal.

Our oldest son had a similar problem as a teenager. But, like most doctors' kids, he didn't get much attention paid to it. After we suddenly realized that this child had a problem, we had him use castor oil regularly on the mosaic wart—and it was gone shortly. It has neither stopped him from (nor aided him in) becoming an orthopedic surgeon.

Scalp Problems. Another of our correspondents told us the following story, and backed it up with pictures. Phil's mother was disturbed the day after he was born because of a knot on his head about the size of a golf ball. The pediatrician assured her that this was not unusual—"Newborns' heads look funny," was his remark. However, each day the size of the tumor grew larger, until the doctor finally X-rayed the child's head, found it to be most likely a hematoma (an accumulation of blood under the scalp) or a hemangioma, which is a series of very small blood vessels that proliferate to form a red spot or a red lesion on the skin. He told the mother that it would continue to grow until he was age one or two and that nothing could be done until then. The mother continues the story:

> The swelling grew daily—the growth was noticeable and my concern grew, being a new mother. My mother . . . called me in Iowa one day

and said to try the castor oil packs. (At that time, the tumor was almost the size of his head.) The next day I started them—by that evening I thought the tumor was getting smaller, but then I thought it might be my imagination, too. By the next afternoon it was definitely noticeable that it was going away. I continued the packs for five days and the swelling was gone, except for a very small knot that disappeared in three weeks. His doctor was amazed and took several pictures of the "after" and requested pictures of the "before."

I have seen the pictures of the child at three weeks and again at six weeks, and they are remarkable. The mother told me one more thing. She said her pediatrician "laughed when I told him of the castor oil packs." His reaction reminds me of what other doctors have said following the successful administration of castor oil packs on a case they describe as "stubborn." They usually say, "Well, some patients get well no matter what you do to them!"

In the readings, Edgar Cayce suggested the use of the packs for more serious conditions than identified here—these are for the most part creative applications of a principle to the healing of the body by those who have that investigative instinct.

Why does it work so well for such a variety of conditions? Until our research has been completed, we won't have a complete explanation. But we have developed some theories based on what Edgar Cayce said and what we have observed in our practice. One theory is that the oil, when absorbed by the skin into the tissues, carries some remarkable therapeutic property to the afflicted areas and thereby expedites the natural healing process. A second theory is that the oil, when applied to the skin, acts as an energy conductor, delivering healing vibrations from outside the body to the afflicted organs. And of course, both may be true.

The mechanism of its healing power may one day become obvious, but we have some information currently available that helps us toward understanding. The first stages of our research into the use of these packs not only gave evidence that castor oil packs actually improve the functioning of the immune system, but indicated how they aid physiological processes, as seen by the sleeping Mr. Cayce. (See Harvey Grady, "Research into the Mystery of Castor Oil," in

Proceedings of Twenty-first Annual Medical Symposium, A.R.E. Clinic, Phoenix, 1988.) Forty-two times he indicated that eliminations would be increased. The packs would stimulate the liver—this was mentioned in forty readings. Thirty different organs, systems, symptoms, diseases, or conditions were referenced as being aided by these packs. It was recommended for dissolving and removing lesions and adhesions, relieving pain, releasing colon impaction, reducing nervous system incoordination, stimulating the gall bladder, increasing lymphatic circulation, reducing inflammation, increasing relaxation, and many, many other uses.

As we put castor oil packs to the test in clinical medicine over the years, we found that the basic actions that resulted from application of packs to the body fell into two major categories. One was increasing the flow of the lymphatics and the action of the lymph locally where the packs are applied. This led us to understand that the immune system was being aided, since the lymphatic system is the immune system, including the thymus, of course, the tonsils and adenoids, the lymph nodes, the liver, spleen, and bones, the Peyer's patches, and the appendix.

Thus, small packs over puncture wounds and larger packs over an inflamed appendix fall into the same physiological category. A woman who had developed abcesses in the lymph glands of the axilla (armpit) avoided surgery by placing castor oil packs on the area intermittently over a period of two weeks. In a series of some twelve patients who had clinical appendicitis (in the early stages), all but one avoided unnecessary surgery. These were all my patients, and the one whom I sent to surgery was a woman who didn't really think it was going to work.

Many times I have seen fingers that were smashed, with blood under the fingernails, normalize after application of bandages soaked with castor oil. Bruises clear up much more quickly when castor oil is merely rubbed into the area. Skin becomes more youthful in appearance when massaged gently at night before retiring. Teenagers with acne and older women with wrinkles all appreciate this response. The point of all this is that such results could not come about unless the lymphatics underneath the skin—and sometimes deep within the body—are influenced to become more active in their immune response.

The second major category of response is the relaxation of the body. Relaxation is a neurological response, affecting the entire nervous system of the body. One of the most common responses to the application of packs over the abdomen is the report that "I slept better" or "It made me so relaxed." When an organ functions more normally in relationship with another organ, it is logical to assume that much of the response to therapy is in the autonomic nervous system, where most tensions reside.

Our research has not come to the point of understanding how castor oil on the skin of the abdomen can affect the solar plexus, for instance, in a tranquilizing manner, but this is what we have seen, and the explanation is still in the future. Perhaps the vibration of the atoms in the oil send a message to those atoms that make up the organs within the body—a message of peace, perhaps, placing on the afflicted part the hand of the Christ.

Cayce said, "Remember, life is vibration." Everything vibrates. It is undoubtedly true that the vibration of a healthy body is different from that of a sick one. Illness or disability or disease are a manifestation of a disturbance in the normal vibrations of the body. So, one way or another, castor oil may be an agent for restoring the body's natural vibratory pattern. How it does it is a mystery.

It remains obvious, however, that this is one tool that not only works physiologically to bring about healing in the body but carries with it the principle that identifies Edgar Cayce's medicine for today—the awakening power to the cells and the forces deep inside the body. They are being called upon to wake up, to recognize the source of all healing within.

PART III

Healing Your Mind

14

An Adventure in Consciousness

WHAT IS IT THAT causes people who experience these individual healings with the use of castor oil packs to get so excited that they want to share it with their families and their friends and help them to get healed too? Is it simply the spirit of the adventure?

I recall when David, the youngest of our six, was playing with a neighbor boy in our backyard when he was eight or nine years old. They apparently found some old pieces of glass and the other boy cut the palm of his hand. It wasn't bad, David thought, so he took it upon himself to fix it up. He picked an aloe vera stalk, trimmed off its rough green skin—as he had seen his parents do many times—and then cut off a piece of the gelatinous interior portion of the plant sufficient in length to cover the cut. Then he bandaged it up with a piece of cloth.

We knew nothing about it until we got a call from the emergency room of the local hospital. "Doctor," said the unfamiliar voice, "can you tell me what this green stuff is that your son put on this boy's hand?" Well, all's well that ends well, and it did. The boy got his hand sutured up; there was no infection; and the boys and their parents remained friends.

But think what an adventure those two boys had. David knew about the healing quality of aloe vera, and his first instinct was to take care of his friend who had cut his hand. Is it any wonder that David ended up becoming a doctor?

Isn't it wonderful to go into a cave that you've never seen before? Or to explore a mountainside? Or look into the face of the lowly dandelion plant—as I did when I was a boy—and wonder what it contains that can bring healing to the body? Isn't it the same kind of wonderful adventure when we contact information that leads us to understand that *all* things are possible for us and then go about healing one part of ourselves with a very simple remedy? Doesn't it thrill a certain part of ourselves and say, "Hey, I'm *really* like that—I *can* do anything!"

Donna June must have felt like that as she was going through her adventure. Between 1963 and 1971, she had two surgical procedures done to clean out the inside of the uterus, which had been bleeding severely: "In May 1971, I was diagnosed by two doctors (one an osteopath and the other a gynecologist) to have a fibroid tumor the size of a baseball in the wall of my uterus. The osteopath recommended that I have a hysterectomy by July and not to put it off. My gynecologist confirmed the presence of the tumor but suggested another D&C." (A D&C is surgery to dilate the cervix and curette the inside of the uterus.)

Edgar Cayce had once recommended using Glycothymoline and Atomidine douches, alternating them regularly, for a woman who had a fibroid tumor. Donna June tried this, but found she was sensitive to iodine, so she discontinued these. Meanwhile another doctor advised her to start castor oil packs instead, applying them over the lower abdomen.

> I was too busy to work with the packs until August 1. I began using the packs every morning at 5:00 A.M. for one hour—then I would get up and go to work. I did this for one week. I had started a period again on the day I was to be examined by my gynecologist. She remarked that I had an unusual amount of mucus and she scheduled surgery for the end of August. I awoke that night, however, and found that I was flooding again, heavily.

She couldn't get into the hospital immediately—no beds were available—but was finally admitted forty-eight hours later and taken to the operating room immediately. Her story continues:

> When I came to, I felt wonderful and hungry. I asked my doctor about the tumor and her answer was "There was no tumor." I asked her if a fibroid ever just cut loose and came out and her answer was a definite "Never!" I felt by her emphasis that she would not appreciate my idea of what happened to the tumor. Her explanation was that there had been a mass of clots and a misdiagnosis. So be it.
>
> Out of this treatment, I received a bonus. I had had some gall bladder flareups and after using the castor oil packs, I have not had any reoccurrence of that problem either. Since all of the above happenings, I have gone through menopause and feel that, if it were not for the packs, I would be minus my female organs right now.

We can't prove that the castor oil pack was responsible, but wasn't her healing—however it happened—exciting? She certainly caught the awareness inside herself that good things can happen to her body. And, at any time, the adventure can begin.

Not as exciting, but just as impressive, was the experience of a sixty-five-year-old man with rheumatoid arthritis. He came to the Clinic with a three-month history of typical rheumatoid swelling of his right foot and ankle. He had also recently developed back pain. His latex test for rheumatoid arthritis was reported positive.

His regimen of therapy followed closely those suggestions Cayce gave for this condition: Atomidine in series and in cycles, epsom salts baths each week, full-body massage to be followed by local massages with peanut oil on his foot and ankle each night before retiring, visualization techniques, and an arthritis diet.

His response was rapid. In two months, the swelling was gone; there was no discomfort and no stiffness; and, to all intents and purposes, he was well once again. His mind had been open to the wonderful healing qualities of the body.

When Edgar Cayce was in his mid-thirties, his wife contracted tuberculosis. The one therapy that allowed her to return back to normal was inhaling fumes of applejack brandy from an old charred oak keg. In the years since Cayce first used that treatment, it has brought remarkable responses for a variety of cases.

One patient who was afflicted with chronic bronchitis and emphysema was eager to try something different, so we recommended that Dan try inhalations from the charred oak keg with apple brandy in it. He responded very satisfactorily. His breathing became easier, and he had no more respiratory infections, which cause difficulty for emphysema patients.

Dan was so regular in using this therapy that he carried the oak keg in the backseat of his car to his job in the field. In Arizona, the field means desert country, where it gets quite hot. When his supervisor visited the job site one day, Dan had to go to his car to get his job plans. His boss followed along, and when he opened the back door of his car, the pleasant odors of brandy wafted out on the breezes.

"Dan, you cannot drink on the job!"

"Boss, I don't drink that stuff, I just smell it!"

"Sure, Dan!" his boss said skeptically.

It took a letter from me to get Dan off the hook.

It seems to me that there are many factors that make up an adventure—whether it's an adventure in consciousness inside a person, or one out in the world we live in. One has to be the enthusiasm with which one faces all the passing events of life and turns them into adventures. Enthusiasm makes an adventure out of what starts out to be a trip to the grocery store. One day our five-year-old Bob trailed along behind his oldest brother; they were simply going up the street a way. When they returned just a few minutes later, Bob was breathless. Carl had found the whitened skull of a small animal in a ditch, and they were relishing the event. Bob kept saying, "Boy, what a 'asperience! Boy, what a 'asperience!"

Frank McKibbon apparently had that sort of enthusiasm for life. Every five years he sends me his observations on what the new events in his life have brought him. He has now finished his ninety-fifth year, and was aiming at one hundred when last I heard from him. When he was "nine decades, moving toward a century," he wrote these lines to his family and friends and shared them with me:

I don't deserve all this. Yet, it just may be a sort of pay-off, the pay-off of fine parents, a good home, a happy boyhood, hard work—plowing sod from sunrise to sunset, pitching hay and wheat, digging telephone pole holes; active youth—hunting, baseball, basketball and football; later—yard work and gardening, remodeling houses into comfortable homes; challenging and creating vocational activities; happy marriage, wonderful wife, children and grandchildren; retirement, sixty-five years in the ministry; and now ninety! Still reading and writing, fishing and (sometimes) jogging—how utterly simple, and yet, for me, what a life!

Never have I been more interested, excited, and eager than at this moment. I hope for time to share with others, particularly my children and grandchildren, the story I am writing, "Pilgrimage of a Seeker," describing "where I am" in my thinking and "how I got that way"; possibly my eighth book. The pilgrimage has been long and slow, with much struggling, lots of surprises, keen joy, and tremendous gratification.

I hold that the fundamental process of the universe—God's method of creation and procedure—is *evolution*. With human beings it is continuing change, growth; physical, mental, emotional and spiritual. I am part of that process. How I have evolved in my few years! And how I hope it has not ended, on this plane, nor will it on the next, or the next?

Frank's adventure obviously has been accompanied by the joy of living and by the excitement and enthusiasm of expressing his creative abilities. And to express that much enthusiasm when one is ninety is great. His "evolution" reminds me of what Cayce said about the direction that Frank has obviously taken, for Cayce's viewpoint portrayed each entity, each soul, as in a process of awakening to its purpose and to its goal of oneness. He saw Frank's kind of evolution as a growing experience with the understanding that those constructive influences placed in the lives and experiences of others produce growth in one's own relationships to creative energies. And Cayce said, "For only with the purpose held in that direction may there be the vision of the glory that is prepared for those who seek to know His Face" (no. 1463–1).

People looking for adventures in healing are not only enthusiastic, they are willing to do something that might help, and their minds are open to the wonders of their own body. A nurse wrote me a letter telling of the experience she fashioned for herself. Kathryn's ailment was physical, but her approach was expectant:

> In November, while squatting and twisting to reach something in the kitchen, I injured my right knee. The pain was terrific, and the swelling made walking difficult. A week later I was able to see an orthopedist in New Haven.
>
> He stated that the knee cartilage was completely torn and that I could not injure the joint further by activity, and that treatment was symptomatic. If the joint continued to be swollen and painful, surgery to remove the cartilage could be performed with a possible remission of symptoms. As a nurse, I was more than reluctant to submit to surgery, especially since my brother had had this same problem, which surgery only partially alleviated.
>
> In January, my mother gave me her copy of Jess Stearn's book *The Sleeping Prophet*, about Edgar Cayce. Since I have dry skin, I made a lotion of peanut oil, olive oil, lanolin, and rose water (as Cayce suggested) and it did help the dry skin condition. I started massaging it into my knee after I read also that peanut oil will decrease the incidence of arthritis, which I expected would add to my discomfort as time went on. By this time, I had a well-established limp, and I had accepted it as the way I was going to walk for the rest of my life. (I am twenty-six years old.)
>
> One month previous to the injury, I had started jogging two miles a day, but after the injury I couldn't walk well, let alone run. After about a week of half-hearted daily massages to my knee, I noticed that I was not limping all the time any longer, but only after prolonged standing and walking, which my job requires. In two weeks of almost daily massages with the lotion, I felt up to walking the two-mile route I had previously run, and by March 1 was running the entire distance in 13 to 17 minutes.
>
> At first my knee hurt very badly, but it hurt walking anyway, so I ran. Then gradually I could forget that I had a knee, and just enjoyed running. This was a fantastic development, since I had resigned myself to a lifetime of a "bad knee," the same as my paternal grandmother and

aunts have suffered most of their adult lives. I am currently running three to eight miles a day with only occasional discomfort in my knee. The limp has resolved, and there has been no swelling since March.

Kathryn might indeed have read also a reading given by Edgar Cayce about the use of peanut oil. He told of that particular oil's very specific action on the circulation and "structural forces." Massage with peanut oil creates in the circulatory system the influences that make the skin, muscles, nerves, and tendons more pliable as they relate to the bony structure of the body. And, through the radiation and absorption effect of the oil, the bones themselves are strengthened (no. 2968–1).

Jack might have finally read the same extract in the readings. He had trouble, not with his knee, but with his shoulders.

In 1974, before I became acquainted with the Cayce concepts of healing, I suffered an accident. I developed a severe case of traumatic arthritis in both shoulders as a result of the accident, and a cervical spondylitis in the second and third vertebrae.

I had surgery on one shoulder, and the orthopedic surgeon, the neurosurgeon, the orthopedic-neurosurgeon, and my Dr. Jones, who worked with the orthopedic surgeon, all agreed that I would never be able to use my arms to amount to anything, ever again. They were right—for seven years.

After I began reading about the Cayce treatments, I began using peanut oil and an infrared lamp. In about four months, I noticed I had a little more range of movement in my arms and a little less pain. From then on, I slowly but steadily improved. Today my shoulders are almost healed and my neck is considerably better.

Jack's adventure in healing brought him from a state of partial disability back to near normal—a real life-changing experience. He wasn't the only one in his family to benefit by applying Cayce's simple suggestions. He wrote that his wife "cured the corns on her toes in ten days with baking soda and spirits of camphor, after our family doctor and family surgeon told her that the only way she would ever get rid of them was through surgery. So . . ."

What Jack's family doctor and family surgeon told her ended up as empty words. The problem with such prophecies—for that's what they were—and what makes doctors such lousy prophets is that the data that has been published about such illnesses does not consider the will of the individual and the healing powers inherent in each person, waiting to be activated.

This is probably the best reason to ask your doctor the next time he or she espouses a prophecy for you, "Upon what is this prognosis or prophecy based?" And then you need to look for the physician within and ask that power just what is going to happen. This will always be a better source of information.

It is always difficult to tell which ailments are truly minimal and which are very important, for little things can grow. One of my first experiences was with an insignificant puncture wound on my hand, after I had trimmed the date palm trees in my yard. I thought nothing about it at first, but by the second day it had grown into an angry, inflamed infection.

Because of my belief that castor oil promotes the flow of lymph in the tissue on which it is places, my immediate reaction was to rub it with castor oil two or three times that day, then put some castor oil on a bandage and wrap my hand that night. The next morning the inflammation was almost gone. I massaged it with castor oil another three or four times that day, forgetting the bandage that night, and the next day, my hand was normal.

Whenever we have anyone with a puncture wound, our first suggestion is to use castor oil at the site of the injury. That's not the only treatment in the Cayce books, however. In Dr. Harold Reilly's *Handbook to Health Through Drugless Therapy*, a treatment for an insect sting consists of applying a salt pack to the swollen area. This reduces both the swelling and the pain.

What is the touchstone here, the common denominator that is to be found in the minds and bodies of all these people who have experienced just a little or a larger reprieve from injury or illness because of something most often very simple? For all these experiences provided relief from applying something simple: castor oil, salt, peanut oil, olive oil, lanolin, rose water, applejack brandy, iodine, epsom salts, food, Glycothymoline, vibrations from the infrared lamp—all these things are relatively simple, and they are to be found in nature, too. Cayce had specific opinions in his readings about the value of natural healing. He said we really have available from nature not only a correction for every illness the human frame encounters but also an antidote for every poison. He added that nature is really the counterpart of the mental and spiritual realms, so illnesses can also be brought under control by activities of the mind—suggestion, hypnosis, visualization—or through prayer or the laying on of hands, for instance (no. 2396–2).

I recall another reading, which indicated that you can cure most any condition, but you can't cure a hard-headed, stiff-necked old man! What that was saying to me was, no matter how much of the good in nature we apply to the body, it will do no good unless one is open and ready to allow an awakening of one's consciousness to move further toward healing and one's real destination in life.

Thus an adventure in consciousness may not be—probably *cannot be*—a single step, as in overcoming an injured thumb or rheumatoid arthritis. Every journey really starts with the first step, and those who experienced the joy of discovery, the new awareness of their bodies, have taken that first step.

They have experienced the enthusiasm, the touching of the world within, the recognition that they do have a real choice in how they live their lives, they have learned that they *can* care for their bodies themselves and that their minds can be open to the wonders of the world profitably and with joy and the feeling that they have—in a small way—overcome the world.

15

Medicine for Today

W HEN I WAS JUST beginning my medical school training, I remember the great discussions other medical students and I had as we worked on our cadavers in anatomy lab. They often centered on the numerous ways in which people end their lives on this plane. We were speculating on what kind of illness or accident we would prefer to die from—appropriate for a pathology laboratory, right? One student said he'd like to go in his sleep from a heart attack. Another said, "Any way at all, but I don't really want to get old and decrepit." Someone else said, "To die young rather than old and decrepit isn't exactly my choice!" I don't recall what opinion I voiced, if any.

It was obvious, however, that all of us at that stage of our understanding felt that the disease was inflicted on us and that we didn't really have a choice.

I'm not sure what medical students talk about today. But we *do* have a choice. We can choose illness or health, at least to some degree. We need to recognize that fact and then do something about it. We are at that period in time when we know what to do but still find it hard to accomplish the goal.

In the Temple Beautiful programs, people come with a variety of problems and questions, but they have already had that awakening of consciousness that tells them they have within these bodies a spark of life that needs only to be stirred up into a flame, and the illness will be gone. Somewhere along the way, they have had that "aha!" experience, the application of a salt pack on an insect bite or a castor oil pack on a sprained ankle that says to them, "This is a mystery in life itself, and I love mysteries. Let me at it!"

Once that knowledge comes that something constructive can be done about any condition of the body, then one is off and running, ready to make headway in this thing that we call illness, which, I *always* tell them, is simply the result of them breaking a law of the body or the mind or the spirit. That's what Cayce called sin—the going down a path that we chose to take without considering our true nature as an eternal soul and our deepest desire to make our wills one with the creative Source of the universe.

One of the readings that underlies what I think of as Edgar Cayce's medicine for today speaks of our true nature and our eventual destiny—what healing is all about anyway. "The first cause was," it said, "that the created would be the companion for the creator, that it, the creature, would show itself to be not only worthy of, but companionable to, the Creator." Cayce went on to say that every form of life is "an essence of manifestation of the Creator; not the Creator, but a manifestation of a first cause, and in its own sphere, its own consciousness of its activity in that plane or sphere" (no. 5753–1).

It is really that we, being created in the image of God, are on the path toward what we call a oneness with him, but we do not see the path well at all most of the time. So we stray. Well, that venture off the path gives us difficulties, which call our attention to the reality that it is not exactly easy to get along here in the rough. So we search for and find our way back again.

The difficulties most often are correctly identified as karmic; that is, we meet what we have meted, or we reap what we have sown, or we look at ourselves in a mirror. We can look at it several different ways, but in the end it is simply the Creator's love in establishing ways that we can choose to get back on that old path we have vacated so often.

There are two ways to keep ourselves on it. One is to listen to the wisdom that has been given us over the centuries—God speaking, in a very true sense. Jesus said to love God and love your fellow human beings; that's the law and the prophets. Simple, isn't it? By doing that, we stay on the path. But who can find anything in a Hitler to love? Oops—there we go again. For God did indeed create Hitler, as he created the rose that you tenderly smell and love for its fragrance and its beauty. So it's off the path again.

The second way to stay on the path is the law of cause and effect: karma. It kicks us where it hurts, for we cannot love without being loved in return and we cannot hurt another without being hurt sometime in the future. But it does call us back to the path. Yet we don't get there automatically; we have to choose to take the lesson to heart and rearrange something inside ourselves so that we have actually changed. If we do not do so, then we have chosen to go to grade two and take the harder lesson, probably without adequate preparation.

This is really where we are—all of us—somewhere along the way either on that path that takes us back to where we originated or just stumbling through the brambles of life, finding it tough going and wondering where McDonald's is so we can get a hamburger and a cold drink. That, my friends, is real karma. But, take heart, we can always change directions, really, because each of us has been given the power to choose, and most of us today are awakening to that reality and have started the process. We *are* choosing!

When I look up at the sky after it's been raining and I am cold and chilly and wet and I see a patch of blue, I know that something good is going to happen and the sun will shine again very soon. I found a reading that was like that patch of blue, for it told me that being out in the brambles and looking for McDonald's is not so bad, because we can see the patch of blue at that instant and magically change the hamburger and drink into the Path of Life itself. How can this be done? By choice, of course, and acting on it. If we choose to meet those karmic influences by following the path of the Christ, then by our thoughts and deeds and acts, we manifest gentleness and kindness and love and the rest of the fruits of the spirit to our fellow human beings day by day, and the promise is given then that no karmic debts from any other experience or lifetime appear in the present that might not be actually washed away. In other words, by our choice we change direction, and the karma then, which is a lesson to be learned, is no longer affecting us because we have learned the lesson. The lesson is, obviously, to love our fellow human beings and to love God (no. 442–3).

Karma, then, ends up being the manner in which we choose to meet our own actions that have taken us away from where we intended to go in the first place. Strange, isn't it, that we create circumstances in which we fight with ourselves? Because it's not really someone else that we criticize, for example, it's that attitude that we have foisted on others sometime in the past. We are always meeting ourselves, and we do it in interpersonal relationships or in the hardship or illness that calls us to attention. Illness particularly becomes meaningful, because we find the errors of the past showing up in the physical body. And illnesses often symbolize what kind of mental or emotional problem we instituted. But healing comes as we recall and put into action the qualities found on the path of love that we have chosen.

Karma, then, can be obliterated by simply loving. Love in action means being kind when you want to kick someone in the behind. It means smiling when you'd like to call someone a nasty name. Or it might mean being patient with your kids when they slam the door for the hundredth time after you've told them, "*Do not* slam the door!" for the ninety-ninth time.

It's funny, in a sense, especially when we can sit back and take an overview of what goes on. We must do that, moreover, if we are going to find the humor of the situation, and it always is healing when we can laugh.

It is much more difficult to laugh, however, when illness is life-threatening or completely debilitating and wrecking one's ability to cope with life or if it requires the full attendance of loved ones, just to stay alive. It is at times like that, that the laughs are too often few and far between. Yet it is still necessary that we look for that patch of blue. For it will not always rain.

A mother brought her twenty-six-year-old son to the Clinic for treatment under our Brain Injury Program. Born with cerebral palsy,

Sam was unable to communicate and could not swallow. He had a tracheostomy tube in place and a gastrostomy tube for feeding. His mother told Eileen, director of our program, "At one time I had Sam riding a bike." His doctor had put him on a medication that she believes was detrimental. "He could not sit up, and he would not listen. Sam wound up having massive seizures," she said. "He could sing and talk before that. I've never stopped working with him since he was a baby. This is just awful that he has to have all these problems to live with, but I watch over him just as God wants me to."

For years this lovely woman, full to the brim with faith, has cared for her son, and she tries everything she can find to help him move back to normal. How does she find that patch of blue? And how does he find it? It may be simply in being patient, finding a blessing in what others would consider a hardship. It is difficult to understand, but true: this mother is sowing happiness in caring for her son who has such a severe problem. But he finds improvement at the soul level as he works with his mother.

In one of his admonitions to those who care, Cayce had this to say:

> And what is the first law? Like begets like! For in the act, as in the seed, is the fullgrown blossom of what you do, what you think, what you are! Hence, if you sow Happiness will you reap turmoil? or riot? Rather in the still small voice, do you find the song of Happiness, the blessings of divine love directing, guiding, keeping your ways.
>
> What matter if there is no dress, hat, shoes, or even the house rent paid? They are of the moment. If you are happy that you are alive, you still have the opportunity to say, "Blessings be on thee," and these are what live forever. Shadows pass. Only the light and truth lives on. Disturbances and distresses pass. For you say, "God is in His holy temple, let all the earth keep silent." What do you mean? Is it just a saying because you have heard it oft, or do you really believe it?
>
> Then, as His children, *act that way!* (no. 262–109)

Among the many things that I have made part of my life is the admonition that I picked up somewhere in the Cayce readings that "the try is held to Him for righteousness"—not the success, but the try. And, I asked myself, try to do what? I answered, saying, "It is 'the try' to follow that path that I've been talking about. No matter how many times you fall down, no matter how many times you are unsuccessful, no matter how many times you goof up and create a mess— as long as you keep yourself heading in the right direction, all is in order."

I really believe that God loves us in spite of our failures, not because of our goodness. He knows that we have that power of choice that he gave us when we came into being. He knows that we can use it or abuse it. He knows that the life on earth gives us the opportunity to use it constructively and to love significantly enough that we will find our way, our path, again and return to be a companion with him. He knows our inherent goodness.

And the love that is part of each of us is what keeps Sam's mother caring for him and doing all that she knows to make him happy. And she continues to "watch over him just as God wants."

We continue to communicate with her because such problems call us to practice Edgar Cayce's healing art, and to be kind, to be patient, to be caring, to be sensitive to her needs as she cares for her son's needs. And, at the same time, we offer them our best to help in the rehabilitation program.

Recently, Sam's seizures worsened significantly. We suggested using the castor oil packs not only on the abdomen (which was a primary therapy in the readings for epilepsy) but also on the head. Some innovative members of a rabbi's congregation in Israel had started using castor oil packs on the head for conditions such as strokes or cancer of the brain. They are not yet sure of what benefit is to be gained, but they feel the results are promising. So Sam had packs on his head an hour at a time three times a week, and the grand mal seizures are nearly gone. He still cannot talk and sing as he did earlier in life, but he is improving bit by bit. How do we know what's going to happen? That kind of answer cannot be formulated.

Creating Beauty in the Temple

Our residential programs are unique (probably in many ways), especially in that we set up the same kind of therapy program no matter what problem individuals bring with them. In one program, for in-for instance, the diagnoses we were given to work with included cancer, Parkinson's disease, obesity, enlarged heart, osteomyelitis, arthritis, multiple sclerosis, epilepsy, anxiety depression, chronic back problem, and drug abuse.

How do we go about creating beauty in these different temples? We have twelve or fourteen people there in the orientation session, all strangers to one another (but *starting* to break down the ice), and all having hopes and dreams intermingled with real, hard questions: Why am I afflicted with this problem? Why me? What am I *really* here for? What do you mean, goals? What is healing, anyway? Why do you mention death when I'm trying to live? and What are we going to do to get me over this problem?

First, of course, we ask them what they really *expect* out of the seventeen days they will spend here. What do they really *want*? Some find that hard to clarify. They may say, "I just want to get well!" Some want deeper insight, having already faced the question of what life is about anyway and wanting to get on with it.

As this kind of thing goes on in the orientation briefing, individuals start relating to each other. Then, as the days pass, they find deeper and deeper rapport being established between them, and people start helping people. This is perhaps the key to the group sessions. Strangers become brothers and sisters from past lives or workers together who accomplished noble (or ignoble) goals. Some of the oneness gets established that lets them either consciously or unconsciously recognize that they indeed are one with each other, and thus in greater attunement with God. This becomes strong as they progress through the movement, color, and music sessions and the dream interpretations at breakfast time.

Then they help each other as their life stories are shared at dinner, and each little bit of assistance makes for greater beauty in the "temple."

Aches and pains are aided or cleared up as they receive massages or acuscope treatments or chiropractic manipulations. And the emotions that have caused difficulty begin to surface, to be worked with, to be released in the counseling sessions or during guided imagery or visualization while investigating their own unconscious on the ETA.

Stresses are relieved; hates are resolved; anger is softened to create beneficial energy. Within the body's cells and organs, the forces that reside there are awakened to their divine potential.

I've often wondered, "How many cells are enlightened when I meditate for ten minutes? Or when I release a long-held grudge?" My answer, of course, has to be a guess. But I say to myself, "What does it matter, McGarey? Maybe twenty-five cells, may twenty-five hundred! You'll never know, anyway, so why be so picky? If you put your nose and your head and your body in the right direction, you'll get where you want to go. Patience is the key to it, so don't become impatient!"

As our patients think about these things, their bodies receive the kind of physical care that is needed. Their diets are adjusted, and lab tests are taken to find out what more might be needed. As time passes, taking with it the consciousness the patients brought with them, their emotional/attitudinal makeup changes. They grow.

No change, obviously, can take place against the will and the desire of the individual. And some people come to the programs without the willingness to really let go of what they have been carrying for several incarnations. These cases are uncommon, fortunately, and most participants move forward, beautifying the temple as an ongoing activity. Cayce described in one reading (no. 1527–1) how those deadened portions that characterize difficult experiences from past incarnations are aroused to a new awareness. He said one needs to keep the mental and spiritual attitudes that are part of the divine purposes for which an entity comes into the world. Then gradually there develops cooperation between the different parts of the body, a coordinating of the forces, in a sense, and a growth in consciousness where there was depletion and deadening of activity before. In other words, the positive activities that are constructive and creative overcome the habit patterns that in the past have created difficulties.

The beautifying of the temple comes about bit by bit. But it really happens, and with it, sometimes, comes a complete clearing of the problem that existed. We get excited watching it happen, but think of the excitement that must come about in the individual in whom it really takes place.

It took place in Stella Andres, who has since written a book, *Stella* (with co-author Brad Steiger), about her battle with asthma, gangrene, and lymphoma. This is her story in short form, as she wrote it for us, but the excitement we felt as she lived through this in her Temple Beautiful Program (and later) escapes her abbreviated account:

In 1979 I hurt my toe getting out of the tub, and the sore would not heal. I went to a specialist in New York who said I had no pulse in my leg, and after examining me, he said that I had an aneurism on my femoral artery. I went for a second opinion at N.Y.U. Cornell Medical School with the same diagnosis. I was really frightened! The specialist admitted me into a hospital in New York, where they found I had lymphoma—the fourth stage—and not an aneurism. While they were busy with tests my toes turned black. When they removed the toes, the gangrene had progressed so they had to amputate twice more—once below the knee and once above. I was constantly given drugs and was hallucinating. After the third amputation I woke up one morning and two toes on my other foot were black. I decided this was not going to happen again—I took over.

My husband brought me castor oil and gauze. I packed my toes in castor oil and refused all medication and worked with biofeedback and visualization. The doctors advised my husband to get me a wheelchair for a double amputee. I gave them a hard time since I was no longer afraid and wouldn't listen to them, and continued my holistic ways.

In the meantime, I was in touch with the Clinic for support and as soon as the stitches were removed, George and I came to Phoenix. That was March 1980, and with all the support I got from all my friends here at the Clinic and the people in the Temple Program, I was completely healed within six months. I had a very bad asthma attack, which I feel was the catharsis that released the ending phase of all my illness. I haven't had asthma for about four years now. I feel that attack helped heal the little bit of lymphoma left, and my toes healed within six months. I'm fine now and intend to stay that way. I lead a normal life and do everything but run, but then I never did run much. After much hard work my prosthesis fits comfortably, and I hate to remove it even when I go to bed.

Stella had been a patient at the Clinic for asthma prior to the onset of the gangrene. During her stay at the Clinic, she had overcome most of her problem with asthma. During her stay, she made many friends and subsequently created a holistic support group here at the Clinic, which, after the lymphoma was cured, reached people across the country.

Stella really aroused those "deadened portions" in her body, didn't she? She took charge, started exercising her power of choice, and *knew* that she could return that body back to normal. And in the process, she brought exceeding beauty to her own temple. She made it a Temple Beautiful.

Another remarkable case was that of Luke, who was born a Down's syndrome child. Luke did not go through one of our programs, but his presence around the Clinic grounds—either making friends, for medical care, or the ETA treatment with his mother—led to his becoming such a favorite with everyone who knew him that he finally got a pin that he wore proudly: "A.R.E. Clinic Luke McClary Boy Wonder." For he was really that.

Luke was fortunate in having two parents and siblings who loved him so much that they moved from Australia to the United States in order to get treatment for him, in the form of a program of neurological organization from the Institutes for the Achievement of Human Potential in Philadelphia. They settled in Phoenix, where they practiced as chiropractors, and eventually brought Luke into the Clinic for help.

At first he was for the most part flaccid, hardly able to take nourishment. He made some growth gains, but not much. Then, later on in 1979, he was started on treatments with the ETA, which seemed to bring changes into his body as the electromagnetic fields did their job.

In March 1980, he was reevaluated at the Institutes in Philadelphia, and his growth was remarkable as his body sought to catch up with other kids his age. In the seven months that had passed since his prior checkup, Luke's head grew at 750 percent of the normal rate; his chest grew at 333 percent of the norm; and his weight increased more in those seven months than it had in the previous year and a half. There was significant improvement also seen in his motor control, mobility, and language. His handicap, rated as "severe," was remarkably lessened as Luke gained in many ways.

He started to walk, learned how to read, and became a favorite around the Clinic. Luke gradually approached the growth pattern of a normal child. His weight, head size, chest size, and height all were responding better than expected under normal treatment. As he grew and flourished, his "tag" as a Down's syndrome child was pushed into the background by everyone who knew him.

His development was so good that he underwent successful heart surgery to correct a congenital defect that contributes to the early death of many of these children. His happy disposition and awareness were landmarks that suggested that he was more and more becoming a fully normal child. Thus it was a blow to all of us who loved him when, months later, Luke's heart gave way, and he moved on to a new environment, his job here done. The cause of death was recorded as myocardial failure, the heart muscle not being able to keep up to its accustomed job.

An autopsy showed that Luke's brain had been developing consistently with that of a normal child of five years. Because the brain is the dominant organ in establishing one's ability to function normally, the healthy development of Luke's brain indicated his movement out of the state that we call Down's syndrome.

Luke, the A.R.E. Clinic Boy Wonder, was really that. His response to a program of neurological organization, including patterning, the Cayce remedies, chiropractic treatments and electromagnetic field therapy, as reported by Harvey Grady in 1982 in the *Journal of Holistic Medicine* (4:2), had been truly remarkable from all measurements and parameters that were available. He absorbed all the love that was offered him and gave back more. Whatever his genetic disturbance was, I am sure it changed as he grew and prospered. In the short period of time that he spent in this dimension, Luke demonstrated that, no matter what the condition of the physical body, changes can always come about that spell healing in the long run. No one can look into another's heart and tell what his or her life purpose is, but I feel confident that Luke fulfilled his this time around, and his parents gained a great deal of love and healing in the process of helping Luke.

Future Promises

As each of us starts his or her journey into the rest of this incarnation, we should be mindful of the seven rules of healing, based on the wisdom of Edgar Cayce. They are indispensable to our progress. If we ask ourselves these questions and answer them honestly, our prospects for healing in body, mind, and spirit will improve:

1. **Do I know what healing really is?** Remember, healing may come through changes in our mental attitude, or spiritual influences such as prayer and the laying on of hands, as readily as through the surgeon's skill. It may come through corrections in our diet or the use of herbs or such unconventional medications as castor oil or the aroma of applejack brandy. For as Cayce put it, "all healing comes from the one source. And whether there is the application of foods, exercise, medicine, or even the knife—it is to bring the consciousness of the forces within the body that aid in reproducing themselves— the awareness of Creative or God Forces" (no. 2926–1).

2. **Have I really the desire to be healed?** Desire-power, or motivation is the energy that propels people toward success of all kinds. It is what Stella had in overcoming her near-fatal afflictions. Cayce indicated that the human desire for a purposeful life is mandatory. As he put it, desire will boost the lymph system through the sympathetic nervous system "as much as all the doses that may ever be given" (no. 2456–6). Without it, he said, little may be accomplished.

3. **Do I expect to be healed?** Expectancy is an essential element in healing. An expectant attitude is as important as any therapy. It involves the proper relationship to the power of the healing forces in the universe, or as Cayce said, "All healing of *every* nature is the attuning of the body to the Creative

Forces of the Divine within, by whatever means may be used to coordinate physical, mental, and spiritual" (no. 2348–3).

4. **What is my purpose in being healed?** Everyone has the power to choose his or her purpose in life. And whether that choice is made before or after we are born, it always has to do with the soul's advancement to fulfill its destiny. And the soul's progress is intimately related to the healing of the body, to the miracle of regeneration. Cayce said that "each word, each act, each hope, each element of activity is to be selfless and unto the glory of Creative Forces, or God" (no. 2994–1).

5. **What can the doctor do to bring healing?** Your doctor may or may not understand that all healing instruments, methods, modalities, herbs, medicines, and chemicals, as well as the energies that come from his or her hands and presence, are manifestations of the Divine. Cayce would draw a distinct line between the true healer and those who call themselves doctors. Cayce put it like this:

> To be a physical healer or a physician of the material body, without a knowledge of the mental body, and without the ability to apply the spiritual force, there is expended just a part of a healer, and a healer for dollars and cents. Heal for that of making the body one with the whole (no. 2739–2).

6. **What can I do to bring healing?** Follow the injunction: apply the truths known; do what you know best to do. Cayce suggested that to know what to do and to do it not is a violation of the rules of healing. It detours us from the spiritual path that leads to healing, to wholeness, to oneness with God. He also said that when truths are applied, we discover greater truths. "Only by application—even if by rule or rote—may you find the true meaning of laws" (no. 967–1). Cayce reminded us to be open-minded and openhearted, to forgive and to forget.

7. **Do I accept the challenge of being healed and becoming whole?** This challenge of becoming whole confronts every-

one, no matter how sick, no matter how well we think we are. For we all need healing in a portion of our being. We need to make choices that will bring healing into our lives. We need to do it with love in all its aspects, and to reap the fruits of the loving spirit—faith, hope, kindness, gentleness, patience— and thus transform our own bodies into what we can call the Temple Beautiful. That is really what personal healing is all about.

We were all created by a loving God who wants us to be aware of our individuality, to cherish the unique qualities that make us distinct from everyone else, and yet to recognize that our destiny is to be one with him. Today the world and all its nations, families, and individuals, all of us, are going through that transformation. We see the sickness around us in individuals, in relationships between people, between religious groups, between nations, and we feel the need to bring peace and harmony and goodwill. Healing is the key, healing of body, mind, and spirit.

I believe that it is our destiny to be healed, to be whole, to know joy. The healing energies required to bring about these miracles are within us. We have all witnessed them, from the disappearance of an angry bruise or laceration to the mending of a fractured bone— everyday miracles that we take for granted, but miracles nonetheless. The challenge for us is to make the choices in our lives that will allow healing to happen. We are more influential than we may realize, and the challenge of Edgar Cayce's wisdom for the New Age is to recognize that we can become a healing influence wherever we go. The healing of the world begins with the healing of one person, no matter where that person is. It begins with you and with me.

APPENDIX

CASTOR OIL PACKS

Materials Needed:

1. Wool flannel cloth
2. Plastic sheet, medium thickness
3. Electric heating pad
4. Bath towel
5. Two safety pins

Instructions for Use:

Prepare first a soft flannel cloth (cotton flannel is all right if wool flannel is not available) that is two to four thicknesses and measures about ten by twelve inches after it is folded. This is the size needed for abdominal application. Other areas may need a different size pack. Pour some castor oil onto the cloth. Make sure the cloth is wet but not drippy with oil. Then apply the cloth to the area that needs treatment.

Next, apply a plastic covering over the soaked flannel cloth. On top of that place a heating pad and turn it up to "low" to begin with—then to "medium" or "high" if the body tolerates it. Then wrap a towel, folded lengthwise, around the entire area and fasten it with safety pins. The heating pad should remain in place between one and one and a half hours *only*. The pack itself can be worn all night. Be extremely careful to avoid excessive heat! The idea is to help, not hurt.

The skin can be cleansed afterward by using soda water (to a quart of water, add two teaspoons baking soda).

Keep the flannel pack in a plastic container for future use. It is possible to use the same pack for different problems, and it need not be discarded after one application, but check with your physician about specifics. *Do not attempt to clean pack.*

DIET BASICS FROM THE EDGAR CAYCE READINGS

Remember . . .
There is as much of God in the
physical as there is in the
spiritual or mental, for it should
be one! (no. 69–5)

. . . never, under strain, when very tired, very excited, very mad, should the body take foods in[to] the system . . . and never take any food that the body finds is not agreeing with same. . . . (no. 137–30)

. . . have rather a percentage of 80% alkaline-producing to 20% acid-producing foods. Then, it is well that the body not become as one that couldn't do this, that or the other; or as a slave to an idea of a set diet. Do not take citrus fruit juices *and* cereals at the same meal. Do not take milk or cream in coffee or in tea. Do not eat fried foods of any kind. (no. 1568–2)

. . . when there is the tendency towards an alkaline system there is less effect of cold and congestion. (no. 270–33)

Do not have large quantities of any fruits, vegetables, meats, that are not grown in or come to the area where the body is at the time it partakes of such foods. This will be found to be a good rule to be followed by all. This prepares the system to acclimate itself to any given territory. (no. 3542–1)

. . . cereals that carry the heart of the grain; vegetables of the leafy kind; fruits and nuts. . . . The almond carries more phosphorus *and* iron in a combination easily assimilated than any other nut. (no. 1131–2)

Include in the diet often raw vegetables prepared in various ways, not merely as a salad but scraped or grated and combined with gelatin. . . .

(no. 3445–1)

Q. Please explain the vitamin content of gelatin. . . .
A. It isn't the vitamin content but it is ability to work with the activities of the glands, causing the glands to take from that absorbed or digested the vitamins that would not be active if there is not sufficient gelatin in the body.

(no. 849–75)

Do not use bacon or fats in cooking the vegetables. . . . (no. 303–11)

Plenty of lettuce should always be eaten by most *every* body; for this supplies an effluvium in the bloodstream itself that is a destructive force to *most* of those influences that attack the bloodstream. It's a purifier. (no. 404–6)

Do have plenty of vegetables [grown] above the ground; at least three of these to one below the ground. Have at least one leafy vegetable to every one of the pod vegetables taken.   (no. 2602–1)

Corn and tomatoes are excellent. More of the vitamins are obtained in tomatoes [vine ripened] than in any other *one* growing vegetable.
                                                                 (no. 900–386)

Yet if these [tomatoes] are not cared for properly, they may become very destructive to a physical organism; that is, if they ripen after being pulled. . . . The tomato is one vegetable that in most instances . . . is preferable to be eaten after being canned, for it is then much more uniform.
                                                                 (no. 584–5)

. . . olive oil in small quantities . . . as it is a food for the intestinal system. . . .   (no. 543–26)

. . . do not eat great quantities of starch with the proteins or meats.
                                                                 (no. 416–9)

Avoid too much of the heavy meats not well cooked. . . . The meats taken would be preferably fish, fowl, and lamb; others *not* so often. Breakfast bacon, crisp, may be taken occasionally.   (no. 1710–4)

Q. How much water should the body drink daily?
A. Six to eight tumblers or glasses full.   (no. 1131–2)

Bolting food or swallowing it by the use of liquids produces more colds than *any one* activity of a diet! Even milk or water should be *chewed* two to three times before taken into the stomach. . . .   (no. 808–3)

Well, then, each morning upon first arising, to take a half to three-quarters of a glass of warm water . . . this will clarify the system of poisons.
                                                                 (no. 311–4)

The cooking of condiments, even salt, *destroys* much of the vitamins of foods.   (no. 906–1)

Certain characters of food cooked in aluminum are bad for *any* system. . . . Cook rather in granite, or better still in Patapar paper [vegetable parchment paper].   (no. 1196–7)

Q. Consider also the steam pressure for cooking foods quickly. Would it be recommended and does it destroy any of the precious vitamins of the vegetables and fruits?
A. Rather preserves than destroys.   (no. 462–14)

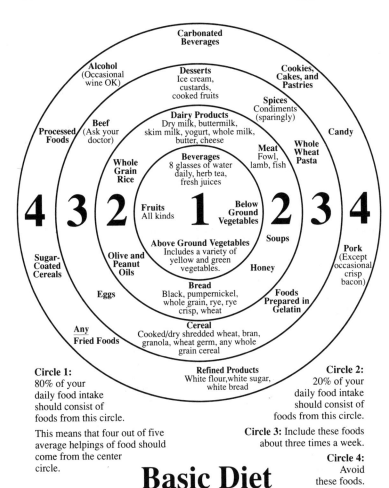

Carbonated
Beverages

Alcohol
(Occasional
wine OK)

Desserts
Ice cream,
custards,
cooked fruits

Cookies,
Cakes, and
Pastries

Spices
Condiments
(sparingly)

Processed
Foods

Beef
(Ask your
doctor)

Dairy Products
Dry milk, buttermilk,
skim milk, yogurt, whole milk,
butter, cheese

Candy

Whole
Grain
Rice

Beverages
8 glasses of water
daily, herb tea,
fresh juices

Meat
Fowl,
lamb, fish

Whole
Wheat
Pasta

4   3   2

Fruits
All kinds

1

Below
Ground
Vegetables

2   3   4

Sugar-
Coated
Cereals

Olive and
Peanut
Oils

Above Ground Vegetables
Includes a variety of
yellow and green
vegetables.

Soups

Honey

Pork
(Except
occasional
crisp
bacon)

Eggs

Bread
Black, pumpernickel,
whole grain, rye, rye
crisp, wheat

Foods
Prepared in
Gelatin

Any
Fried Foods

Cereal
Cooked/dry shredded wheat, bran,
granola, wheat germ, any whole
grain cereal

Circle 1:
80% of your
daily food intake
should consist of
foods from this circle.

Refined Products
White flour, white sugar,
white bread

Circle 2:
20% of your
daily food intake
should consist of
foods from this circle.

This means that four out of five
average helpings of food should
come from the center
circle.

Circle 3: Include these foods
about three times a week.

Circle 4:
Avoid
these foods.

Basic Diet

MENU SAMPLES

BREAKFAST
Citrus fruit or cereal.
(Do not combine these at
the same meal.)
Boiled or scrambled egg
Whole wheat toast
Glass of milk

LUNCH
Have a completely RAW
lunch and/or vegetable soup,
Include green leafy
vegetables in a
combination salad with oil
dressing or mayonnaise
One slice bread and butter
Beverage

DINNER
Meat: Fish, fowl,
or lamb
Cooked vegetables
Include a variety of
above and below
ground, yellow and
green vegetables
Dessert if desired
Beverage

Developed by the physicians, nurses, and staff of the A.R.E. Clinic, Inc., Phoenix, Arizona

THE ACID–ALKALINE BALANCE*

Alkaline-Forming Foods

All fruits, fresh and dried, except prunes, plums, and cranberries.

Apricots	Limes
Berries	Oranges
Dates	Peaches
Figs (unsulphured)	Pears
Grapefruit	Pineapples
Lemons	Raisins

All vegetables, fresh and dehydrated, except legumes (dried peas, beans, and lentils) and rhubarb.

Asparagus	Olives (ripe)
Beets	Onions
Carob	Oyster plant
Carrots	Parsnips
Cauliflower	Radishes
Celery	Rutabagas
Eggplant	Spinach
Green beans	Sprouts
Kohlrabi	Sweet potatoes
Lettuce	Tomato juice
Mushrooms	

Milk, all forms: cottage cheese, cheese.

Honey

Acid-Forming Foods

Vegetable oils

Prunes, plums, cranberries, rhubarb

---

*Food lists taken from *Edgar Cayce on Diet and Health*, by A. Read, C. Ilstrup, and M. Gammon (New York: Warner Books, 1969). See also Arthur W. Snyder, *Foods That Preserve the Alkaline Reserve* (Los Angeles: Hanson Publishing Co., 1972).

All cereal grains and their products
All high-starch and high-protein foods
Nuts: almonds, filberts, almond butter
Legumes: dried beans, dried peas, lentils
Meats: Lamb
Poultry: chicken, turkey, guinea hen, duck, goose, wild game
Visceral meats: heart, brains, kidney, liver, sweetbreads, thymus
Egg whites (yolks are not acid-forming)

Never when under strain, very tired, very excited, or very mad should the body take foods into the system. And never take any food that the body finds is not agreeing with same. (no. 137–15)

We are, physically and mentally, what we eat and what we think. (no. 288–38)

ARTHRITIS DIET

Basic Principles

1. Eat liberal amounts of fruits and vegetables—fresh if possible, frozen or dried second best. Include a large raw vegetable salad as one main meal daily. Combine raw vegetables with gelatin often.

2. Watch acid-alkaline balance.

3. Avoid certain food combinations.

4. Balance foods grown above and below the ground—3 above to 1 below. Eat more leafy vegetables than pod-type.

Do Not Eat

1. White, bleached, or refined flour or grains or products made from these processed grains.

2. Refined sugar, raw sugar, brown sugar, molasses, or products made with it, such as jams, marmalades, ice cream, pastries, or candies.

3. Chocolate.

4. Milk or cream (very small amounts of milk allowed).

5. Pork (including bacon), beef, or veal.

6. Fat, especially animal fat.

7. Fried foods.

8. Canned (tinned) foods.

9. Spices or highly seasoned food.

10. Alcohol.

11. Beer, malt drinks, or carbonated water (soft drinks).

12. Cabbage or starchy foods.

13. Apples, bananas, strawberries, or fresh tomatoes.

These Foods Should Be Included in Your Diet

1. All kinds of raw vegetables (except cabbage): especially watercress, chard, mustard greens, kale, carrots, celery, lettuce (leaf or romaine).

2. Use only whole grain products. Black bread in moderation (pumpernickel, rye, or whole wheat).

3. Nuts, especially almonds and filberts. (Raw nuts are better than those roasted and salted).

4. Fish and seafood, fowl, lamb, wild game, liver, tripe, and pig knuckles (the only exception to no pork).

5. Vegetable juices, citrus fruit juices at times when cereal is

6. Berries (except strawberries) and citrus fruits.

7. Cooked leafy vegetables (except cabbage), pieplant (salsify), parsnips, potato peelings from the baked potato but not the bulk of it.

8. Jerusalem artichoke once each week. (It is a root.)

9. A great deal of watercress and beet tops. (These especially help the eliminations.)

10. All fruits (except apples, bananas, and strawberries), preferably fresh.

11. Sweet milk and buttermilk in small amounts occasionally.

12. Small amounts of honey.

13. Use a vegetable seed oil or peanut oil.

14. Small amounts of black coffee or tea, as permitted by your physician.

15. Small amounts of cheese and two or three soft-cooked or poached eggs per week as permitted by your physician.

Avoid Food Combinations Such as

1. Citrus fruits with whole grain products.

2. Coffee or tea with milk and/or sugar.

3. A large quantity of starch combined with meat (protein) or sweets (fruits).

Acid-alkaline Balance

Some foods are acid forming when eaten and others are alkaline forming. The diet should be adjusted so that the proper balance is maintained in the body. The right balance is 80% alkaline to 20% acid. In order to obtain an 80% alkaline balance in your diet, four out of every five helpings should come from the alkaline-forming foods list.

DIET FOR ECZEMA

1. No fried foods. This includes potato chips, corn chips, and the like.

2. No carbonated drinks. This includes diet drinks, beer, and ale.

3. No candy, sugar, pastry, pie, ice cream. Honey may be used occasionally on buckwheat pancakes.

4. No potatoes or white bread. Limit starches to 20% of diet.

5. No pork, beef, or ham. For meats use lamb, fish, and fowl prepared by baking, broiling, or stewing.

6. No butter, greases, fats. No oily salad dressings.

7. Vegetables should be a substantial part of diet. Carrots, okra, squash, and the like are especially recommended, also fresh green salads (but without oily salad dressings!). Avoid peas and dried and baked beans, however.

8. Fruits: Eat only sparingly. Avoid raw apples and bananas.

9. Mullein tea: Every evening at bedtime drink a cup or more of mullein tea. This may be obtained at a health food store. Prepare by placing about one-half teaspoon in a cup and pouring boiling water over it. Allow to steep for thirty minutes, strain, and drink.

10. Avoid heavy seasoning in foods.

11. Milk, eggs (yolks only), and cheese are all right.

12. It is suggested that you do not combine citrus fruits and cereal at the same meal.

SELECTED
BIBLIOGRAPHY

A Search for God. Virginia Beach, VA: Edgar Cayce Foundation, 1987.

Cayce, Gail. *Osteopathy*. Virginia Beach, VA: Edgar Cayce Foundation, 1973.

Jesus the Pattern. Virginia Beach, VA: Edgar Cayce Foundation, 1980.

McGarey, William A. *Edgar Cayce Remedies*. New York: Bantam Books, 1983.

———. *Physicians Reference Notebook*. Virginia Beach, VA: Edgar Cayce Foundation, 1968.

Montgomery, D. W. "Castor Oil." *J. Cutaneous Disease*, 36 (1918): 446.

Oulette, R. *Holistic Healing*. Fall River, MA: Aero Press Publishers, 1980.

Read, A., C. Ilstrup, and M. Gammon. *Edgar Cayce on Diet and Health*. New York: Warner Books, 1969.

Rusznyák, Istv'an, et al. *Lymphatics and Lymph Circulation: Physiology and Pathology*, edited by L. Youlten. 2nd English edition. Elmsford, NY: Pergamon Press, 1967.

A Search for God. Virginia Beach, VA: Edgar Cayce Foundation, 1987.

INDEX

ABOUT THE
AUTHOR

William A. McGarey is a family physician and an author or co-author of eight books. In 1970, he and his wife, Gladys T. McGarey, M.D., began the A.R.E. clinic in Phoenix, Arizona. He is also a founding member of the American Holistic Medical Association and a lecturer on holistic medicine.

In 1965, Dr. McGarey was appointed Director of the Medical Research Division of the Edgar Cayce Foundation and has been instrumental in activating research programs designed to evaluate concepts in the Cayce readings as they pertain to physiology and therapy. Because of his familiarity with the Edgar Cayce readings, Dr. McGarey has lectured and taught for the Association for Research and Enlightenment in conferences, workshops, and lecture situations throughout the United States.

EDGAR CAYCE'S
WISDOM FOR THE NEW AGE

More information from the Edgar Cayce readings is available to you on hundreds of topics, from astrology and arthritis to universal laws and world affairs, because Cayce established an organization, the Association for Research and Enlightenment (A.R.E.), to preserve his readings and make the information available to everyone.

Today over seventy-five thousand members of the A.R.E. receive a bimonthly magazine, *Venture Inward*, containing articles on dream interpretation, past lives, health and diet, psychic archaeology, and psi research, book reviews, and interviews with leaders in the metaphysical field. Members also receive extracts of medical and nonmedical readings and may do their own research in all of the over fourteen thousand readings that Edgar Cayce gave during his lifetime.

To receive more information about the association, which continues to research as well as make available information on subjects in the Edgar Cayce readings, please write A.R.E., Dept. M13, P.O. Box 595, Virginia Beach, VA 23451, or call (804) 428–3588. The A.R.E. will be happy to send you a packet of materials describing its current activities.